"If you want one
year of prosperity,
grow grain ...

... If you want 10 years of prosperity, grow trees ...

... If you want 100 years of prosperity, grow **people**."

CHINESE PROVERB

CONTENTS

PART 1

THE LIES: Bogus Buzzwords and Baseless Best Practices We Believed

PART 2

THE PARADIGM: The Simple Truths That Motivate Us All

PART 3

THE PROCESS: Say Goodbye to Expensive Turnover

KEEP THEM LONGER

EXCLUSIVE MINI COURSE

An on-demand solution to go beyond the book, start reducing expensive turnover today, and discover plug and play templates for immediate use.

Go To: KeepThemLonger.com/offer

Get laser-focused solutions proven to create exceptional cultures that last. Redeem this exclusive offer for the official Keep Them Longer Mini-Course.

KEEP THEM LONGER

Phil discovered his passion for helping people by pulling a gun out of his college roommate's mouth.[1]

Today, Phil is a human resources manager at a major grocery chain. He's in his thirties with an average height and disarming smile. If Phil weren't wearing a corporate logo shirt, you'd probably find him in a polo shirt tucked into his neatly pressed jeans. Now, Phil isn't the most outspoken person in the room. He prefers answering questions to asking questions. We spent the day with Phil and his team, when he brought up an upcoming move to Arizona—where he will help build out a new division of the company.

He is one of the thousands of people who have sat in one of our training sessions. In our sessions, we get to the core of an individual's purpose fast. Why do we spend so much time in our employee engagement training on purpose? Because most employers only leverage one part of their employees' purposes. They essentially ignore the other parts that are essential to keeping them longer.

Before getting started, we asked the group to discuss only what they felt comfortable sharing. Phil was one of the first to go through the process. We went through the process of discovering his purpose and applying it to his work (you can find *The PurposeFinder Formula*™ in Chapter Nine).

We asked Phil, "What is the #1 event in your life that changed the way you see the world?"

What followed left the room without words. When Phil was in college, he had an unconventional roommate. They were friends, but not close. Phil was the upbeat, always-in-a-good-mood kind of guy. He's the type that shows up before anyone else with coffee and a bag of pastries to share. His roommate was shy, awkward, and moody. One day, walking back from class, Phil had no idea that he was about to walk in on his roommate's attempted suicide. As he opened the door to his apartment, Phil found his roommate with that gun in his mouth, about to take his own life.

Phil rushed over—no panic, no judgment—and helped pull the gun from his roommate's mouth. In the weeks and months that followed, Phil helped his roommate find a reason to live. He helped him get a job and checked on him regularly. Phil made sure his friend got the help he needed. He said that moment helped him discover that he wanted to help people find meaning in their work.

There wasn't a dry eye in the room.

Out of this group of 10 human resource leaders, not one had heard Phil's story before. Most of them had worked with Phil for at least three years, and yet, not one of them knew the incredible life moment that shaped his entire career. On that day, something powerful happened in that training room. A team of coworkers went from merely working together to doing life together.

YOUR PEOPLE NEED TO KNOW THEY MATTER

Every single person in your organization wants to be seen. They want to be heard. They want to know that they matter. We didn't understand this principle ourselves until about five years into our business. We were young entrepreneurs making all of our rookie mistakes. We made it all about the product, selling until we couldn't sell anymore, and counting the dollars and metrics instead of counting the number of transformed lives and companies. Don't get us wrong. That produced incredible success.

We spoke on big stages, helped the most prominent companies, appeared on national television, and even made a couple of trips to the White House—all before the age of 30. Our team was growing, and it seemed that we had finally hit our stride. Then it all stopped. Loyal clients stopped returning calls. Promising leads fell off the map. Momentum screeched to a painful, embarrassing halt. We would go weeks without a single closed deal and months without any direction. Our sales team was quitting on us, and the rest of our staff started looking for other jobs or playing video games on their company laptops. It was bad.

LIFE TRANSFORMATION IS THE SECRET

Then came an email from a close friend and university president. Attached was a lesser known interview transcript between 20 nationally respected journalists and Rick Warren, author of the #1 bestselling hardback book in U.S. history, *The Purpose-Driven Life*.[2] Rick Warren is an author and a pastor, but he was also directly mentored by the late management expert, Peter Drucker. In reading this massive interview transcript, we were about to learn our greatest business lesson to date—and it had nothing to do with business.

Rick said two things in the interview that we'll never forget:

1. "I'm in the transformation business…. What motivates me is that I am addicted to changing lives. Everybody tries to attribute the growth of churches to everything else but what makes them [actually] grow—and it's changed lives."

2. "When people's lives are changed, you'd have to lock the doors to keep them out, because they want to go where their lives are changed."[3]

There it was, our life's turning point.

The real secret to organizational growth is transformation. From that day forward, we set our focus on transforming as many lives and companies as possible. We would never sell a client until we knew that we could bring transformation to their organization. We would spend more time serving and less time selling. As leaders, we decided that we would give more than we take and expect nothing in return—as long as people's lives were changed.

We knew that the transformation of our mindset was significant, but we had no idea how much. When we focused on giving instead of taking and transformation instead of tallying deals, everything changed. Funny enough, when revenue stopped being our focus, our revenue doubled in the 12 months that followed. That also happened the next year. As we were already in the talent retention business, we discovered something else. Inside this mindset, transformation was also the key to retaining top talent for the long-term. We've since called that discovery the Keep Them Longer method. It's a method that says you must give to your employees long before you take from them. It says, "You must see them first, grow them always, and involve them today."

We immediately put those principles to work at the National Automobile Dealers Association (NADA) conference a few years ago. The automotive industry, like others, struggles big time with keeping talent. If you thought losing employees every two years was bad, imagine losing a sales associate every three months. After delivering the Keep Them Longer method from the stage, we received a message from one of the largest automotive dealers in Australia a few weeks later. Our new Aussie friend had completely restructured his approach to hiring, training, and retaining his team after sitting in on our session. Even his Millennials were sticking around longer and showing all the signs of being fully engaged.

"I must say—the results are amazing!" he concluded.

We noticed a trend. The leaders that were keeping their talent were giving to their workforce first by seeing them, growing them, involving them—and showing them how to give back. They maximized tomorrow by transforming the lives of their talent today. The leaders that were losing their talent did the opposite.

They took more than they gave and expected higher pay and better benefits to be the Band-Aid. Their people left anyway. Productivity faltered. Their brand became tainted.

Most companies only talk about employees being their greatest asset. The Keep Them Longer method is a system that makes it happen.

YES, TURNOVER IS PREVENTABLE

The cycle of recruiting, interviewing, hiring, and then losing great talent happens every day. It happens to big businesses and small businesses. It affects companies that have been around for a hundred years and companies that are newly incorporated. It happens so often, and to so many businesses, that leaders assume it will occur. But it doesn't have to be this way.

Turnover is not only preventable, it is reversible. This book is a referendum against the outdated mindset of treating employees like expenses instead of assets. It is a blueprint for leaders of every age, every industry, and every level of experience to build and lead an organization that people don't want to leave.

So how do companies strategically cut turnover? Can business leaders and managers identify threats to retention before it's too late? We have studied employee motivation and retention best practices for over a decade, specializing in how and why each generation works. The book in your hands is a culmination of hundreds of studies, assessments, case studies, interviews, and solutions we have implemented with clients all over the world.

You are about to discover the time-tested principles proven to work for corner bakeries and international super-brands, whether you're in the United States, Europe, Dubai, or Australia. These principles work if you are brand new at a company and still earning your influence. They work if you are a seasoned executive who sets the budget and direction of the company. They work if you're 22 or 62. In fact, throughout this book, we will give you specific examples of how leaders of varying influence and experience levels have been able to cut turnover and increase engagement.

Our specialization in Millennial motivation has brought us into the executive suites of the world's most recognizable brands, including Safeway, Volkswagen, Comcast, and others. And despite our unique work in Millennial engagement and retention, we found this one principle to be true: What retains your new and young employees will keep everyone else as well.

THIS WILL WORK FOR YOU, NO MATTER YOUR INDUSTRY OR EXPERIENCE

You're busy. You have demanding clients, customers, employees, and bosses. You also have a family and probably one or two hobbies you'd like to spend more time doing. That's why we created the Keep Them Longer method. It is the method that leaders at all levels can implement with their team in seven days or less.

This book is a toolbox of solutions. Not all of the answers will work for you, your company, or your industry. We've given you suggested uses and defined who should leverage them. We also include handy checklists to help you measure how you and your team are doing. We will also point you to additional resources (including courses, online videos, and training) to provide further information for you and your team.

WHAT YOU WILL LEARN IN THIS BOOK

Becoming a better leader starts with becoming a more informed one. We've divided this book into four sections. The first section is foundational to understanding the rest of the book. It gives you the tools that you will use to unpack the remaining chapters. The next section will break down the myths that leaders have come to believe that are limiting their effectiveness. The following section will provide the paradigm to keeping them longer. You'll see where science-backed solutions meet the real-world application. The final section provides you with the specific programs and processes to use within your organization.

We have designed each chapter for the busy leader who is ready for a clear plan to cut turnover. Each chapter ends with a summary of the principles discussed. Plus, you'll see how to apply the principles in three minutes or less. We have done the hard work in distilling the absolute best practices in retention so you don't have to.

This book will equip you with specific skills to do the following:

1. Identify employees at risk of quitting.
2. Create a culture that keeps talent longer at all levels.

3. Determine the areas in your company where retention can be improved.
4. Empower your team to co-create a culture of retention.
5. Develop programmatic solutions that leave a legacy of engagement and fulfillment.

You will also discover the five elements of retention:

1. Recruiting systems that work—no matter your industry or budget.
2. Interview secrets that will quickly highlight the best candidates for your culture.
3. Onboarding best practices that help your new hires discover and apply their purpose.
4. Training programs and systems that grow great leaders.
5. Culture-growing strategies that transform employees into raving fans and corporate partners.

The process of finding and keeping employees is both science and art. With this book, you will have more than confidence. You will know how to cut costly turnover in your company measurably. You will know how to create a complete culture powered by purpose, mission, and fulfillment.

But here's the deal.

You have to do it. The book is not another business book meant to sit in your book cemetery. That's what we call an executive's bookshelf that never gets used. If you read this book and do nothing with the information in it, you might as well not cash in on a winning lotto ticket. Results are only as good as the leaders who make it happen. We will provide you with the tools to achieve incredible feats. You must commit right now to doing what it takes to make your company into a Keep Them Longer culture.

ESSENTIALS TO KEEP THEM LONGER

High turnover is preventable. You can reduce expensive turnover, improve the quality of candidates you hire, and increase the impact of the training your company provides. The foundational principle to Keep Them Longer is to provide life transformation to every single employee, no matter their position or time with the company. To Keep Them Longer, you'll need to take specific, strategic action in that direction. We'll show you how.

THE
WATER
CYCLE
PRINCIPLE

"We turn them loose with a few constraints."
–Andrea Passman, CNX Resources Corporation

Bernard Palissy was fascinated. Born in the early days of the French Renaissance, Bernard joined a world balancing both science and beauty. Bernard was a chemist and a religious reformer. He was a surveyor and a glassblower.[1] On a trip to the Near East, he became obsessed with imitating porcelain and created ceramic plate ware. But he also had a fascination with realism. When he couldn't imitate the bodies of the animals he was seeking to mimic, he began attaching casts of dead lizards, snakes, and insects to his works.[2] His work can be seen at the Getty Museum overlooking the Los Angeles traffic.[3]

Born before the left-brain, right-brain myth, Bernard was a complicated man. He was a devout Protestant, a crime that would eventually lead to his imprisonment and death. Bernard was a passionate artist whose works were curated by the French Queen Catherine de' Medici.[4] He was a curious inventor committed to discovery. Bernard observed what we know as "The Water Cycle." What prompted the French potter and engineer to the discovery were questions like: "How do streams keep flowing without the water running out?" and "Where do underground aquifers come from?"[5]

Bernard's inquisitiveness led to our understanding that the sun heats large bodies of water. The water evaporates, becomes clouds, and falls to earth as precipitation, replenishing rivers, streams, underground aquifers, and glaciers. Then the six-step cycle starts all over again. It is an invisible process of many systems working together to complete a critical mission. One aspect of the cycle cannot survive without its fellow steps. When one is altered, the rest are affected.

The Water Cycle is profoundly simple to explain. You learned it in elementary school, yet it took hundreds of years to simplify. In the same way, the theory of leadership has evolved. Now, we have combined and simplified these approaches in The Water Cycle Principle. Just like the water cycle for our planet, companies have a flow of interdependent relationships. The components are: (1) Leaders, (2) Employees, (3) Customers, and (4) Owners/Shareholders.

Each aspect of The Corporate Water Cycle flows into the next. If a single component of the cycle does not perform effectively, the next group immediately feels the effects. If leaders do not provide value to the employees, the employees will leave or perform poorly. If employees do not provide value to the customers, the customers will stop giving them money. If customers stop providing value to the owners and shareholders, the owners and shareholders will stop investing in the company. If the shareholders don't provide value to the leaders, the leaders will not be able to invest in the employees.

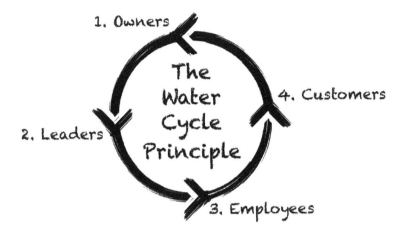

Figure 1: The Water Cycle Principle

Here's how a company that keeps its top talent should function according to The Water Cycle Principle:

1. **Leaders** add value to employees by helping them discover their purpose and showing them how to live it out at work.
2. **Employees** add value to customers by providing solutions for their problems and satisfaction for their needs.
3. **Customers** add value to the owners for the solutions and satisfaction they received.
4. **Owners/Shareholders** add value back into the leaders to make further investments into the employees.

The sun is the conductor of flow in the water cycle. The leader is the conductor of flow in an organization. The leader that fails to give more than he takes stops the flow completely. While the leader is the initial "giver," each participant must give more than he takes for the cycle to continue. If this is done right, the value will flow in the right direction, and the company will grow exponentially. If not, the company will shrink and eventually die.

Here's why: If the leader demands value from his or her employees but fails to pass value down, every stage of the cycle suffers—particularly the customers. When customers feel underserved, they will go elsewhere. Without customers, owners and shareholders don't earn a profit. When the money stops flowing at the top, the leaders have less to draw from to grow their employees because they will be more focused on survival. Here is why companies fail. It is not bad economies. Companies fail because they refuse to understand the principle of The Water Cycle.

EVERYTHING RISES AND FALLS ON VALUE

Andrea Passman, Senior Vice President of Engineering and Operations at CNX Resources Corporation, is a leader who understands The Water Cycle Principle. Founded in 1860, CNX is a billion-dollar natural gas company that hires new engineers right out of school. In the early 2000s, they noticed that the workforce was changing. They had to change if they were going to keep their shareholders happy.

Rather than ignorantly expecting their employees to shift to the traditional way of thinking, CNX did something that very few corporate giants ever do. They changed. They decided to learn from their employees, no matter their age or experience. New engineering employees at CNX get placed in a 15-month rotation in which they can work and observe any part of the company, including legal, finance, and human resources.

During the lengthy onboarding process, new hires are guided through the discovery of their mission and vision. With the employees' personal missions discovered, the company then helps employees connect their personal mission to the company's mission. Following the self-discovery phase, they're guided through applying their personal mission to the mission of the company. The company's mission is: "To empower our team to embrace and drive innovative change that creates long-term per-share value for our investors, enhances our communities and delivers energy solutions for today and tomorrow."

CNX goes beyond simply onboarding and training. The company gets the new engineers involved immediately. Through a program CNX calls "Fresh Eyes," new hires are "turned loose with a few constraints," according to Andrea. They can observe any company process and suggest changes. The proposed changes are then presented to the CEO. At first, the approach seemed unconventional.

Many even questioned if the new hires would have anything useful to contribute. They are fresh out of college, after all. Through gritted teeth for some and open arms for others, the organization launched the program. In one fiscal year, eight new engineering hires produced $12 million in savings to the company's bottom line. That's The Water Cycle Principle in practice—teaching employees how to add value to others and their organization.

T3 EMPLOYMENT

The Water Cycle Principle states that value must pass freely and regularly throughout an organization. Like any organism, a company must have healthy moving parts to survive. But it isn't merely positive value that can pass through an organization's water cycle. Negative value, like fear-based leadership, can also be passed from leaders to employees, from employees to customers, from customers to shareholders, and from shareholders back to the leaders. Value starts with how leaders view their employees.

How leaders view their employees directly influences their ability to keep them longer. Our T3 Employment Model categorizes the type of employee based on how they interact with their employer.

The T3 Employment Model reveals the relationship between a company and employees and includes:

1. **Transactional Employment** - Employees work for security and consistency.
2. **Transformational Employment** - Employees work for the opportunity to transform someone, something, and themselves.
3. **Transitional Employment** - Employees treat their work as a transition between other opportunities.

There is a significant shift in employment going on worldwide. Employees are coming to work expecting faster promotions, more robust benefits, and more convenient access to opportunities. Part of this is due to Millennials entering the workforce, but the expectations bias is consistent across generations. Employers still operating in the old way of thinking will be edged out by more progressive companies willing to make the shift. Employment has shifted from transactional employment to transformation and transitional employment.

Transactional Employment

In transactional employment, employees work for a company because of what the company gives them. That includes the salary, benefits, retirement, or the company car in exchange for their work. This type of employment has been the prevailing mindset of employers throughout the last century. It led to breakthroughs in innovation and fueled industry worldwide.

Samuel Slater is known as the Father of American Industry. Born and raised in England, Samuel was raised on a successful family farm touting the Puritan work ethic. He grew up in the shadow of the first water-powered mill. Samuel started working in the mill at the age of 14 and soon rose to be superintendent of the entire mill. He was smart, quick to learn, and always looking for an angle to become more successful.

He determined that the most significant opportunity for textiles was in America, where there were no manufactured sewing plants. It was illegal to export such machines or their blueprints out of

England. Samuel used his willpower and sheer grit to memorize the manufacturing processes necessary to run the mill down to how the spindle and gears connected. Armed with this mental blueprint of state-of-the-art machinery used for cotton spinning, Samuel secretly emigrated to New York City disguised as a farmworker. He started the first water-powered textile mill in 1793.[6]

What made him hugely successful was his ability to systemize operations. Samuel represented a shift from focusing on scaling his talent to scaling his systems. Samuel modeled his management structure after military order, with clear lines of authority and access. He employed entire families in his factory, including women and young children. He constructed towns around his mills, with housing, stores, and barbershops—anything his workers needed to stay close to work and away from distractions. These towns would soon be called "Slatervilles" and became standard practice in industrialized cities and towns.

This shift in employment moved individuals and families away from apprenticeships and trades and into grueling and often deadly work conditions. This shift would become known as the American Industrial Revolution and the foundation for the modern corporate structure.

Similar to workers in Samuel's factories, modern employees come to work for the expressed purpose of a paycheck. There is an agreement between employer and employee that if they do the work, they will get paid. But the Great Recession, which started in December 2007, altered the universe in a way that very few predicted. Before the recession, employees endured long hours for the benefits, perks, and, most importantly, the retirement plans. After the recession, that motivator was significantly undermined. The steady jobs that employees expected to have until they retired were laying them off. The benefits that made them feel appreciated were drying up. The retirement funds were no longer reliable. Even if an employee kept their job during the crash, they saw their colleagues and friends suffer around them. Fear flooded the workforce and eroded the transactional nature of work.

Transformational Employment

A transformational workforce is a workforce in which employees want to be part of transforming individuals, industries, and companies—and experience personal transformation in the process. The shift towards transformational employment has occurred as the global competition for talent increases.

To transform is to improve, become greater, and experience a significant and noticeable change. Transformation is intentional. You don't hear about someone accidentally quitting smoking or just happening to lose weight. The bigger the transformation, the more intentional the approach required.

In one of Gabrielle's books, *The Millennial Entrepreneur*, she interviewed young executives and entrepreneurs. She wanted to predict the future economy with Millennials in charge (don't worry, it turns out okay). She talked to a young executive who started a popular pizza chain in the mid-Atlantic. His name is Steve, and he is just a few years older than us. She asked him how he was able to lead a company where the employees were so transient (pizza places aren't exactly known for their life-long employees). His answer was simple, and probably one of the most important leadership lessons we have heard from anyone, let alone someone just over 30.

He explained that he knew his employees were going to quit and move on. For some, it would be a few months, others a few years. But eventually, they would all leave. Then he said, "I want to make their experience working here so awesome that they tell their friends and family about it. I want them to be the best recruiters and the best customers we ever have." Then he hit it out of the park when he said, "I know they will leave. But I want them to become a better person while working here, not just a better employee."

That is the essence of transformation-based employment. It is grounded in the principle that you cannot give what you do not have. If you aren't serving your employees, your employees won't provide excellent service. If you don't go out of your way for your employees, your employees won't go out of their way for your customers. Transformational employment empowers every member of The Corporate Water Cycle to transform the next. If it is difficult for you to find great employees, start with creating great employees. Then you will never have a recruiting or retention problem. In the future of employment, everything will rise and fall on the transformation of individuals.

Transitional Employment

In transitional employment, employees treat each job as a short-term or strategic opportunity. According to the United States Bureau of Labor Statistics (BLS), more than 16.5 million people now make up what's called the "gig economy."[7] That's an increase of 5 percent in five years, with every report showing that the trend isn't slowing down.[8] You may already know about the gig economy because of Uber or Airbnb. However, the gig economy is already changing more stable forms of employment as gig workers enter the traditional workforce.

The freedom and flexibility experienced working a short-term opportunity is appealing for most, but not ideal for all. That is why companies are now creating hybrid employment models that provide stable work with the flexibility of freelance. It allows both the employee and the employer to "test out" the working relationship before making a long-term commitment. Gig work certainly isn't a new form of employment, but it has become popular for three reasons:

1. Technology Makes it Easier Than Ever to Customize a Career

If you have a smartphone and a driver's license, you can drive for Uber. Don't have a car? That's okay! There are now short-term leasing and rental programs that allow individuals with low or no credit to access a vehicle. It's not just ride-share apps that are driving the gig economy. The gig economy is now bringing income opportunities to individuals who may have never had access to steady work. Individuals can now be a dog walker, an interim CFO, or an editor on the side. Technology also gives 24-7 access to recruiters and job platforms. Now, even a slightly dissatisfied employee can scroll through jobs online.

2. Millennials and Generation Z Want More Ownership Over Their Careers

Do you remember the "Choose Your Own Adventure" games in the 1980s? They were gamebooks that allowed you to help create the story. That's how many people are treating their careers. Rather than have one career, today's employees are predicted to have up to 12.[9] That means different industries, different types of jobs, and diverse skills to do each. We're seeing younger workers choose temporary work because they want flexibility, fewer expenses, and autonomy above salary. Our social media manager lives in Australia and travels most of the year. We don't care where she lives, and we don't even care how many hours she works. We care about the work getting done (and that she sends us a picture of a kangaroo now and then).

3. The Economy Changed the Trust Relationship Between Employee and Employer

We are years removed from the throes of the recession, but the effects are felt every day in workplaces across America. The recession caused employees at all levels to distrust corporations. Rather than giving blind loyalty to an employer, many people are taking back their careers by having micro-careers. The switch from transactional to transformational and transitional employment means that employees will be keeping their options open.

It may seem like we are favoring one type over the other. We are. But only in the context of the current economy. When you utilize transformational principles with all of your employees, you keep them longer.

ESSENTIALS OF THE WATER CYCLE PRINCIPLE

The nature of employment has changed, is changing, and will continue to change. Your role as a leader is to use The Water Cycle Principle to steward value throughout the organization. How you view your people will directly influence how your people view and treat your customers. When you treat employees as a means to an end, your employees will see customers as a means to an end. When you create a transformational culture, your employees will create transformational experiences for your customers. When your customers have a transformational experience, they will bring more value to your shareholders and owners. When your shareholders and owners experience value transformation in the market, they will continue to invest back in you, the leader, and the company.

THE
SECRET
SEQUENCE

If every company is subject to the same market forces, why do some companies keep their talent longer than others?

Why do companies that pay the highest salaries and provide the best benefits still lose talent at an alarming rate? The answer isn't in what the company does for the employees; it's in what the company does with the employees. The best leaders consider what makes their people feel valued, not just compensated. They give to their talent today to maximize tomorrow. For leaders to win the talent war, they must live out "The Secret Sequence."

THE POWER OF SEQUENCE

If you had told us two years ago that we'd be mostly vegan, we wouldn't have believed you. We know vegans. They always talk about what they don't eat and take every opportunity to share their favorite tofu recipe. We didn't want to be those people. We just wanted to feel better. The journey to eating plant-based did not happen overnight. It occurred as a result of intentional, measured movements toward a specific goal: better health.

After Brian started suffering from an autoimmune disease, our health became a top priority. We researched what kind of diet protocols would facilitate his body healing itself. After countless blogs, studies, and audiobooks, we switched to an anti-inflammatory diet: no dairy, gluten, or inflammation-causing foods. Inflammation is the leading cause of disease in our bodies, so we figured this would be the fastest way to restore Brian's body. We felt great. His condition reversed within a matter of months, and we continued with our new eating protocol.

Almost a full year after Brian's condition healed, his symptoms returned. We began researching again. We started juicing every day, pounding our bodies with two pounds of fresh vegetables. The results were noticeable to our friends and colleagues. The whites of our eyes glistened. Our skin glowed. Our energy was unprecedented, but no change in Brian's condition. We then removed caffeine, a known agitator for autoimmune disease.

This switch was the hardest yet. We opted for half-caff Americanos and soon enjoyed completely decaffeinated coffee. Yes, decaffeinated coffee still has caffeine, but not in the amount that would trigger his condition. Things began improving, but not fast enough. We decided to make the big switch. No animal products, apart from eggs. We would eat beans and legumes, nuts and seeds, and fermented soy for protein. We meal prepped every Sunday for the week ahead and transformed our mindset into treating food as fuel.

Within months, Brian's condition began to reverse. The transition from eating a healthy but inflammatory diet to consuming mostly organic and plant-based foods was a journey. Taking out caffeine became more manageable because we had eliminated bread. Taking out sugar was made less dramatic by the introduction of more fat and fiber. The result was a success because of the power of sequence.

Many psychologists refer to this as "habit stacking." Habit stacking is an incremental approach to adjusting patterns of human behavior over time. Habit stacking is particularly useful for individuals unwilling to change or if the change is too significant to take on all at once. Habit stacking empowers long-term changes by harnessing the momentum that comes with small wins over time.

THE KEEP THEM LONGER METHOD

The results that this book delivers are powerful, but they happen in a sequence. You may not implement everything in this book. You will not accomplish everything at once. It will take time to bring the transformation necessary for your success. Understanding the sequence has been the most helpful revelation for our clients. Once they permit themselves to pursue big goals consistently over time, everything else is more feasible.

So, what is The Secret Sequence to Keep Them Longer?

1. You must **SEE** your employees before you grow them.
2. You must **GROW** them before you involve them.
3. You must **INVOLVE** them before you teach them how to give.

Keeping talent longer is about setting aside what everybody else is doing and tapping into the human psychology of what drives people to become and remain loyal. That's because your employees were humans before they were employees. Like humans, they have human needs.

In a 1943 academic paper, human psychologist Abraham Maslow theorized that humans have levels of needs, each needing to be met before exploring other aspects of their existence. Maslow's theory would become known as "Maslow's Hierarchy of Needs." A victim of abusive parenting and severe anti-Semitism, Maslow used his studies of primate behavior and human interaction to build a robust theory of human activity.[1]

At the time, Maslow was unimpressed by the social psychology of the day. He did not feel it accurately considered the environment in which humans were living. When he introduced his theory, it was deemed to be counter-cultural. What was once marginal and on the fringe is now considered a mainstream understanding of how humans make decisions.

Here are the basics of Maslow's theory. He represented human needs in a triangle with five different levels. The base, or level one, of the triangle represents humans' "Physiological Needs." These needs include the basics for survival: food, water, warmth, and rest. When your core needs aren't met, it is difficult to address a higher need. Have you ever tried to negotiate the price of a car while being sleep deprived or extremely hungry? Your ability to access the decision-making part of your brain is limited when the survival part of your brain is firing. Perhaps that is why car dealerships are proverbial food deserts, apart from the stale vending machine snacks.

Moving up, level two represents "Safety and Security Needs." The needs include the need to be protected from harm. Our desire for physical and emotional protection reflects our need to feel secure. Someone may be safe from physical harm, but if they are emotionally compromised, they are not able to make good decisions.

Level three represents "Belongingness and Love Needs." We all want to matter. Innate within human behavior is the desire to be a part of a larger group. It is how we grow up, how we receive education, and how we survive as a species.

Level four represents "Esteem Needs." We are designed to crave the approval and acceptance of others. More than that, we desire respect for who we are and what we do. When respect is denied, the threat activators in our brains go off. So much so that someone who feels disrespected has the same chemical reaction in their brain as someone whose physical safety is threatened.

Finally, level five represents "Self-Actualization Needs." These needs include our desire to find significance in life. It is the big "Why" question that is in each of us. The need to matter is a uniquely human desire that has been explored by philosophers, scholars, and religious leaders throughout human history.[2]

But Maslow got some things wrong. At least that's what psychologist Dr. Pamela Rutledge said in her paper on the matter. The modern expert in human motivation and technology said:

"[H]ere's the problem with Maslow's hierarchy. None of these needs—starting with basic survival on up—are possible without social connection and collaboration."[3]

Collaboration is key to every aspect of Maslow's model. You need others to create a warm shelter and find food. You need others to fend off attackers and develop a community of belonging. The ultimate act of collaboration? Giving. More on that later.

You must be willing to work and learn with others to achieve your desired result. You must ask questions that yield complicated answers. Maslow also saw the flow of needs to be directional, starting with basic necessities and growing towards self-actualization. But this does not explain why rich people get depressed or why sick people can be happy. It was a simple tool used to describe the complexity of human desires, but it needs updating.

This triangle is the foundation of the Keep Them Longer method. It is arranged in a flow that rotates from left to right flowing from Seeing Them to Growing Them to Involving Them. The model then ends with the ultimate source of retention, Teaching Them How To Give. It is a sequence that must flow in order. If leaders involve their employees without first developing them, mistakes will be made and profit will be lost. If employees are developed without first discovering their unique value at the company, their training will be in vain.

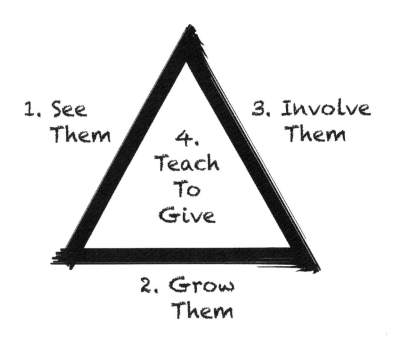

Figure 2: The Keep Them Longer Triangle

If employees are taught to give but don't feel involved in the company, they will not connect their generosity to the organization.

EVERY HUMAN BEING DESIRES TO BE SEEN

"It was actually quite isolating. There were a lot of projections, a lot of assumptions," said Alanis Morissette, the 90s female rock star. The Grammy-winner opened up to Oprah in 2014. She talked about her journey to discover her identity amidst international fame.[4] Her life was a whirlwind. Alanis landed her first record deal at the age of 14. It was another five years before she moved to Los

Angeles and launched her career. Alanis went from playing 200-person clubs to headlining major arenas nearly overnight.

It all happened so fast. Because the iconic rock star became successful so young, Alanis admitted that she never knew who she was. Publicists perfectly crafted her career and handed it to Alanis on a platter. Behind the scenes, she suffered from eating disorders and extreme depression.

The juxtaposition of being recognized by everyone and known by no one is experienced by most in the limelight. The desire to be seen is universal. It goes beyond being recognized. Anyone experiencing international fame would admit being seen goes beyond being famous. It is the desire to be deeply known and loved unconditionally.

EVERY HUMAN BEING MUST GROW AS A WHOLE PERSON

The two most dangerous years in your life are the year you are born and the year you retire. Researchers have determined that you are 20 percent more likely to die the year you retire than any other year of your adult life.[5] And it isn't because of poor health or old age. A similar study found unhealthy individuals still lived longer as long as they stayed working.[6] Why? When you retire, you lose community, structure, and income. But you also lose something else. You lose the environment in which you can discover and grow. The more you learn, the more you find out who you are and how you can improve the world around you.

EVERY HUMAN BEING DESIRES TO BE INVOLVED

Every human being has an innate desire to be in community with others. Researchers like Abraham Maslow refer to this as "belongingness."[7] It's the desire and need to belong. But community is more than just belonging. Community requires participation, authenticity, and interdependence. The higher the stakes, the more critical our ability to rely on one another. The ability to rely on one another is no less true than on the football field.

Bo Schembechler is best known for leading his Michigan Wolverines through 21 successful football seasons, amassing a record of 194-48-5, winning or sharing 13 Big Ten Conference titles.[8] The man was a machine whose passion for the game was only trumped by his passion for the men he coached every day. The College Football Hall of Famer was no stranger to leadership. Bo said:

"If you're going to lead, you need to make goals. And those goals can't come from the top down, they've got to come from the people who are responsible for achieving them. Your job is to help them get there, and remind them every day what their goals are and what they have to do to make their dreams come true.

Sorry, but showing them a slide once a year about what you think their goals should be just doesn't cut it, and it never will. Their goals have to come from them, and those goals have got to be in their bones. Trust your people with that crucial responsibility, and they will never disappoint you. Far from it, they will almost always set the goals higher than you would have ever dared—and then they are the ones who are accountable for their goals!"[9]

EVERYTHING MULTIPLIES WHEN YOU GIVE

When a leader follows the Keep Them Longer method, they grow one of their greatest leadership assets: Trust. Here is what Maslow missed. He missed what the Keep Them Longer triangle represents. It is the fourth step to keeping your talent: Teaching Them to Give. You see, Maslow's Hierarchy of Needs is a relatively self-centered approach to understanding humans. While that's helpful, it misses something pretty incredible.

Giving helps more than the person you assist. Intentional acts of giving are shown to lengthen the lifespan of the giver, reduce risk of disease, and increase self-esteem.[10] And it isn't just money. One study in the Journal of Psychophysiology found that individuals who gave social support to a distressed person significantly lowered their blood pressure.[11] But giving within organizations does not come easily. One of the telltale signs of a toxic work environment is a lack of trust.

Low trust work environments happen because there is not a culture of giving. This dangerous trend can only be reversed when the leaders give first and teach everyone else to do the same. Every human being—if they feel seen, grown, and involved—desires to give and help others. That's because the marketplace is about helping people find solutions to their problems.

We've helped some of the biggest companies in America and the world. In doing that, we've noticed a trend in our employee engagement surveys and focus groups. When you ask employees what they're passionate about, if they don't have a specific answer, they often say, "I'm passionate about helping people." How often do they say that? Two out of three times. We've also found this to be true even in the most challenging and toxic work cultures.

Most of your employees genuinely desire to do more than care for their own needs. If their individual needs are taken care of first, they'll want to help people. If you don't see the desire to help others in your talent, here's why: You haven't executed on three sides of the Keep Them Longer triangle before moving to the fourth step. Later, we'll get more practical as to how you can execute the entire triangle in your organization.

Running a successful company is hard enough. Running a company with global competitors is even harder. To hit goals, post gains, and stay number one requires knowing how to gain, train, and retain top talent. Most people think the answer to that is pay raises, benefits, and more technology. But if you've been in business for any length of time, you may know that the correct answer isn't in what "most people" are doing. It lies within what the "focused few" are doing to keep their talent longer.

ESSENTIALS OF THE SECRET SEQUENCE

Powerful things happen when you follow a process. Imagine making a cake in the wrong order: baking, then mixing, then adding the eggs. It wouldn't work! Following the Keep Them Longer method is essential to your success because it gives you the sequence for success. It is more than paying employees better or giving them more flexible work schedules. The Keep Them Longer method empowers employees in every aspect of their lives. It views employees as multi-dimensional individuals, not just people looking for a paycheck. Employees must be seen before they are grown. They must be grown before they are involved. And when you are ready for them to hit maximum engagement, you must teach them how to give.

PART 1: THE LIES

Bogus Buzzwords &
Baseless Best Practices
That We Believed

4

LIE #1
"We Need More Employee Engagement."

Gabrielle was on her way to present at a conference for Chief Financial Officers just outside of Washington, D.C.

The event was on a university campus. Navigating the packed parking lot and the complicated building was putting her slightly behind schedule. After a few failed attempts at finding the correct lecture hall, she stumbled upon a large lobby with a receptionist desk in the middle. Upon approaching the counter to ask for directions, she found a young woman in her early twenties on her cell phone. She was deep in conversation.

Gabrielle quickly apologized for interrupting but asked if the conference was in this building. The receptionist did not respond but jerked her hand over and pointed at a giant television display showing the events and locations for that day. Unimpressed with the customer service but thankful that she was now in the right place, Gabrielle went upstairs and delivered her talk.

Most of us would consider this young woman a disengaged employee. If I were to ask you, "How do you know when an employee is disengaged?" you would have a list. That list would include: talking on the phone regarding non-work issues, spending time on social media, taking long lunches, not double-checking their work, arriving late, and leaving early.

You wouldn't be wrong.

Employee engagement is a mission-critical pursuit for a leader. According to a Society for Human Resource Management (SHRM) study, executives say that enhancing employee engagement is one of their top five goals.[1] But just because leaders say it's important, doesn't mean it's a priority. According to a Dale Carnegie Research Institute study, only 26 percent of leaders said that employee engagement was an "essential part of what they think about, plan, and do every day." The report found 42 percent of leaders admit that they do work on engagement "frequently." The rest of those surveyed said they work on employee engagement occasionally, rarely, or never.[2]

When employees are engaged, productivity is higher, products and services are better, customers are more satisfied, and profits are bigger.

EMPLOYEE ENGAGEMENT WON'T KEEP THEM LONGER

Knowing all of this, who wouldn't want highly engaged employees? In our work with leaders around the world—and before we take on a company as a client—we ask the leadership, "What's your number one biggest talent problem right now?" Their answer usually includes disloyal or unmotivated employees. Here is our follow-up question: "What do you need to do to fix that?" We use this question to see if they're on the right track or if they need to shift their mindset.

Their typical response to the follow-up is, "We need more employee engagement."

Now that response feels right and sounds right, but it isn't right. It identifies a problem within a company, but incorrectly identifies the source of the problem. More often than not, leaders say, "We need more employee engagement," as if to lay blame on the employees for not being engaged. But employees are only a mirror of their leadership, for better or worse.

If employees are involved, the leadership is involved. If employees are disengaged (and quitting), the leadership is disengaged. So if a leader is struggling to keep his or her talent, it's not an employee problem. It's a leader problem. The longer a leader believes that the employees are the source of the problem, their turnover will get worse. The "we need more employee engagement" mindset is so ingrained in the culture of corporate America that many experts say we're in the middle of an "Employee Engagement Crisis."

That's a lie.

Understanding this lie is the starting point to some of leadership's biggest problems: lack of buy-in, poor performance, low productivity, and, of course, high turnover. So if the "Employee Engagement Crisis" is a lie, then how do you go about re-engaging as a leader so that you can fully engage your employees?

High performers take 100 percent responsibility for both their successes and failures. It is both the benefit and burden of being a leader. The absolute best leaders even take responsibility for actions and omissions they didn't set in motion.

ENGAGEMENT ONLY MATTERS WHEN YOU MEASURE IT

Matthew Watkins is a Senior Director of Enterprise Architecture at Molson Coors. We sat down with him to learn how the American brewing company engages their workforce. Matt is the kind of leader who readily admits that his organization always has room to improve, a telltale sign of an intelligent leader. In our discussion, he discussed employee engagement and customer experience and how the two are deeply connected. When asked about engagement as it relates to retention, Matt said:

> "I think brand loyalty still matters. You have to connect with both employees and customers and show them why they should be loyal. Both groups want to connect with a message and connect with the company behind the message."

Matt agrees that engagement is a process. No engagement efforts will matter without a system in place. The questions discussed at his meetings include, "How do we streamline things?", "How do we automate things?" and, "How do we showcase these elements to new employees in the onboarding process?"

So what does engagement look like for Molson Coors? First, it means discovering the passion of the person entering the company. The company does this by sharing their passion: Beer making. They offer beer-making classes to show employees what the company does and why it matters. Next, engagement includes connecting them to other employees that can best demonstrate the culture of the company.

Engagement could include finding a mentor and meeting people who are aligned with the brand and who personify the values of the company. Finally, Matt believes that authenticity and storytelling are essential to engagement. It seems to be working. Matt admits, "If we look at who stays here long-term, they stay because it aligns with what they want to do in work and life."

At this American beverage giant, engagement isn't just a talking point. Engagement saves money. Highly engaged employees at Molson Coors were five times less likely than non-engaged employees to have a safety incident and seven times less likely to have a lost-time safety incident. By strengthening employee engagement, the company saved $1,721,760 in safety costs in one year alone.[3]

PUT IN PROFESSIONAL EFFORTS TO GET PROFESSIONAL RESULTS

Have you ever attempted to start a new health regime? Maybe it was inspired by a New Year's resolution. Perhaps you didn't like a recent photo of yourself because you noticed some extra pounds. Maybe your doctor said you need to shed some weight or a friend of yours threw down a challenge. All of us have attempted to change our health habits. The hard part is never the goal setting. The hard part is always the execution.

Nir Eyal is "The Prophet of Habit-Forming Technology." The technology investor and bestselling author says that it is impossible to become an expert at something if you use the same effort it takes to become an amateur at something.[4] Let's say you want to have the physique of an action hero. You look up their workouts, what they eat to get the rippling muscles, and how long they were on the program. You wake up on day one, put in the effort, hit your meal plan, and feel great. The same is true on day two through day seven. But then something comes up at home, and you can't make your gym session. You get stressed out at work and you eat a donut, or two, alone in the conference room. At least you didn't take it out of the trashcan.

You try to get back on your regime, but it's hard to find the motivation. How do these Hollywood actors get such great results? You've been doing the same program, and it's taking all of your time and effort; they make it look so easy! Do you want to know the answer? Actors can get ripped bodies in record time because it's their job. They have professional nutritionists, trainers, and chefs, eliminating any excuse for failure. They are the professionals, you are the amateur.

Whether it's how much you can bench press or how many deals you can close, we all want professional results with amateur effort. We want to take a pill to be healthy and download an app to improve our finances. When we try to train like a professional, we give up. It's too hard. The hours are too grueling. There are too many things on our plate. We can't devote the level of effort necessary to get the result we desire. So we stop.

Even the most well-intentioned person falls short of their goals because they didn't match their expectations to their efforts. An amateur fits training into their life. Professionals build their life around their training. If you are not experiencing the engagement transformation within your organization, it may be because you are expecting professional-level results and putting in amateur efforts.

Professionals have systems to be successful. The Keep Them Longer method is the system you will use to improve your culture and your retention measurably.

ENGAGEMENT MEANS TAKING 100 PERCENT RESPONSIBILITY

Not long ago, we came across a video of a young man who challenged himself to work out like Mark Wahlberg. The Hollywood action star gets up at 2:30 a.m. and is in the gym by 4 a.m. To document his progress, this young man had decided to record himself training like Mark Wahlberg for seven days. In the video, you see him groggily getting up, grabbing a coffee, and getting into his car in what appears to be the middle of the night. In the car, he is pumping himself up, explaining to his invisible audience what his workout will include that day. Minutes later, he arrives at the gym promptly at 4:00 a.m. only to find the gym closed. It wouldn't open for another two hours.

He had a choice: Blame his inability to work out on the gym being closed or find a solution. He would have been wholly justified to try again tomorrow or throw in the towel and say it was a silly experiment anyway. But this young man did something many of us rarely do. He took 100 percent responsibility and chose to find a solution. He quickly pulled out his phone. He found a gym that was open just a few miles away, signed up for a membership while sitting in his car, and, in less than 20 minutes, was working out. No excuses. He got it done. Had he chosen to go home, he may have never changed his habits.

Leaders have a similar choice when facing high turnover: Blame the high turnover on the disengaged employees or find a solution. Most leaders today do the former. They blame the employees for not being motivated. They blame the recruiters for bringing in bad talent. They blame the managers for not leading well. They blame the industry for not innovating. They blame the economy for not being like it should. They blame the education system for not adequately preparing young employees. So the turnover continues.

But the best leaders don't skirt responsibility. They take responsibility and find a solution by first re-engaging themselves. They discover their individual purpose and apply it to the company mission. Then, they take action by leveraging their purpose to help their employees experience transformation. They give more than they take and neither blame nor complain about disengaged employees.

EMPLOYEE ENGAGEMENT IS A PROCESS, NOT A PLATITUDE

Talking about engagement and measuring engagement does not improve engagement. The human resources industry is full of articles, videos, TED Talks, and training on employee engagement. Merely talking about it isn't enough. You have to take action. We sat down with Angelia Pelham, former Executive Vice President of Human Resources at Cinemark, to discuss how they engage their workforce. Before our interview, we were taken back to a warmly lit meeting room for the three of us to sit down. After about 15 minutes, Angelia's assistant popped her head in to apologize, but Angelia would be just a few more minutes.

Another ten minutes went by, and Angelia eventually came in and sat down. She apologized profusely for making us wait and explained that she had been up past midnight the night before working the concession stand. "I'm sorry, did you say you were working the concession stand?" Brian clarified. Angelia said, "Yes, every member of the executive team works a movie premiere at least once a year. Last night was my turn."

Cinemark operates over 6,000 screens in the United States and Latin America, and yet its executives make it a priority to stay connected to the core of the business. We asked if this impacted how the executives lead their teams and prioritize their agendas. Her answer was not surprising. "Of course!" she said. When leaders at any level become removed from the service of the organization, the organization's direction and motivation suffer.

DISENGAGED EMPLOYEES HAVE DISENGAGED LEADERS

Engagement starts with the leader, not the employee. A leader can't increase engagement in his or her employees until they first increase their level of commitment. In other words, a leader cannot produce in his or her people what they do not have. So what is engagement? An engaged person is someone who knows their purpose and knows how to connect their purpose to the company mission. They also use their purpose to help their colleagues and customers achieve results.

Engagement is seen, and it is felt.

When Gabrielle had wrapped up her presentation for the Chief Financial Officers, she gathered her things and made her way downstairs. When she got back to the first-floor reception area, she noticed the young woman was still on her phone. This time, she was even deeper in conversation. It was clear this was more than just an employee passing the time with a phone call. Gabrielle decided to walk over and see if everything was alright. As she did, the young woman hurriedly wiped a tear and hung up the phone.

"Is everything okay?"

The young receptionist said that her mother was recently diagnosed with breast cancer in the Philippines. She had tried to get the day off so she could schedule a flight and be with her mother, but no one would take her shift. To the rest of the world, this woman was disengaged and distracted. But the truth was, she was experiencing one of the hardest days of her young life.

Was she engaged at work? No, but we would argue her leaders were not engaging her. When she needed time off to care for her family, she was ignored and rebuffed. Undoubtedly, this young receptionist felt disrespected at work, and her lack of respect influenced how she treated Gabrielle, the customer. Your workforce is made up of people just like this young woman—individuals who will have their best and worst days while working for you. It is your role to model the kind of engagement you expect within your organization.

ESSENTIALS TO EMPLOYEE ENGAGEMENT

Leaders who lean on the excuse of "We need more employee engagement" will never keep them longer. This common corporate buzz phrase feels like progress, but it isn't progress. Engagement is essential, but it is only useful when it is measured. Determine what excellent, acceptable, and unacceptable engagement looks like—and quantify each! If your employees are disengaged, it is a reflection of poorly engaged leaders at every level of the organization.

5

LIE #2
"Better Technology Will Solve This."

On January 12, 2010, a 7.0 magnitude earthquake hit the nation of Haiti.

The quake killed an estimated 230,000 people and displaced at least 1 million more.[1] News cameras swarmed the country broadcasting mothers picking through rubble looking for their children and fathers clinging to their families after their homes were flattened.

To quickly fund operations, the American Red Cross partnered with cell phone carriers to empower Americans to give to the cause with a simple text message. The campaign raised $32 million within days, generating as much as $500,000 per hour.[2] So many donations came in that aid groups could not distribute it all.

A similar text message campaign launched in August of that same year in response to seismic flooding caused by an earthquake in the Middle East. That earthquake displaced 5 million Pakistanis and put another 13 million more at risk of water-borne illnesses.[3] Despite the United Nations ranking the Pakistani crisis more severe than Haiti, the Red Cross's text message effort yielded only

$10,000. That's roughly 0.03 percent of what was generated for Haiti. The same technology was used. Why did one devastating event in Haiti garner 99.7 percent more support than a similar but more severe event in Pakistan?

It had nothing to do with the technology.

Michael Heller is exceptionally passionate about feedback. A human resources professional, he noticed that his organization would talk about feedback but rarely do anything to improve how they reviewed employees. Amid a successful career in human resources, Michael decided to create an app that would enable managers and employees to engage better. The technology is called iRevü and is one of the most popular micro-feedback platforms available. Michael is also a long-time friend.

While catching up over coffee one day, we asked Michael how he has seen his technology change behavior. He said this:

"We can enable behavior, but we can't change it. If a leader doesn't believe that their employees deserve feedback, they aren't going to use our platform, no matter how easy or beautiful it is. We see people going from skeptic to advocate, however, when we show them how feedback increases their bottom line. When we can point to the numbers and say, 'Look how the trust factor has increased,' or 'This is how productivity has gone up,' that makes the difference."

Many leaders experiencing high turnover would love to download an app and make the problem go away. They tell us,

"We need a better operating system," or "We're getting a new Learning Management System," or "We're going to invest in Lynda.com," or "We just need a better communication platform." There are many others, but you get the point.

Many companies believe that they'll be able to solve their high turnover problem with better technology. Companies not only believe that technology is the answer, but they're also putting money behind the false belief. In 2018, 42 percent of companies with more than 100 employees planned to invest in online training systems in 2019.[4]

Now, the last two decades have brought about an explosion of new technologies that companies can use to train their employees and speed up communication. But, over that same period, employee engagement has gone down. In 2017, Gallup reported that 85 percent of employees worldwide are disengaged. When calculated, this disengagement represents roughly $7 trillion in lost productivity.[5]

TECHNOLOGY WILL NEVER REPLACE LEADERSHIP

Turnover, especially among Millennials, has gone up as well. This young generation switches jobs on average every two to three years.[6] Millennials use technology to get degrees, find jobs, and get work done. Technology is more than a convenience. It is a way of life for these young employees. But if technology was the answer, turnover among younger generations should be on its way down.

Technology facilitates communication. It does not promise results. If technology advances and investments were supposed to increase engagement, decrease turnover, and increase employee fulfillment, the results are dismal. And while human resources technology investments have a purpose, they're not the answer to high turnover.

A few years ago, we were speaking at a large conference of California-based Chief Technology Officers. After Gabrielle spoke, the Chief Technology Officer of the California High Patrol (CHP) approached her afterward to share a story. He explained that he was recently working in his office on a Saturday. He didn't typically come into the office to work on the weekend, but he had some emails to return. The office would give him some quiet. About mid-morning, he looked out his office window and saw one of their repair technicians working on the radio tower.

The executive decided to stretch his legs and go outside to chat with the young repair tech. The repair tech was grateful for the break and asked if he could come inside to use the restroom. As they were walking down the hall, the repair tech turned to the executive and asked:

"This may seem like a weird question. But my daughter had a take-your-parent-to-work day the other week. I couldn't go because I was working. But she asked me when she came home from school, 'Daddy, does what you do matter?'"

The executive leaned in close, and then asked, "Well, what did you say?"

The technician turned to him with a blank stare and said, "I told her I didn't know."

The executive couldn't believe it. He asked the technician:

"What do you mean? Your work on our towers ensures they correctly operate so that when someone calls 911 on our highways, the call goes through. When someone reports a car accident or calls for help on the side of the road, your work enables us to dispatch emergency personnel and get right on the scene. What you do saves lives!"

By this time, they had arrived at the restrooms and water fountains. The young repair technician looked at him with tears in his eyes and thanked him. He never knew how his work made a difference. He thought he was repairing radio towers.

What happened there? First, the executive saw the technician by visiting with him where he, the employee, works. Second, the executive grew and involved the technician by connecting his work to the real results of the CHP's work. No learning management system or communication platform was involved in the making of this story. It was real, authentic leadership.

BEING AN EARLY ADOPTER ISN'T ENOUGH

Technology is an amplifier. The latest app may make you feel like you are on the cutting edge, but it may be a Band-Aid for the real problem. Technology can help grow what is good in your organization, but it can also grow what is bad.

Kentaro Toyama explains, "What matters is intent." Kentaro is an ex-Microsoft employee and author of *Geek Heresy: Rescuing Social Change from the Cult of Technology*. Kentaro calls himself a heretic to technocrats everywhere who argue that just adding more technology will be the answer.[7]

But as a computer scientist and an international development researcher, he has seen firsthand that more technology does not equal better results. In his five years of leading Microsoft's research in India, Kentaro discovered one thing to be true. Technology cannot replace leadership. His group did things like connect slum residents to employers, replace farmers' personal computers with smartphones, and create more streamlined testing capabilities for schools. But the success of the programs depended on the partners, not the technology.

That's because technology doesn't address the heart problem. When it comes to organizations, high turnover is a heart problem. It's a human problem. It's a problem in which your employees are saying, "I'm not fulfilled at work." There is simply no piece of technology that can fix that. Only a leader that shifts her mindset to seeing, growing, and involving her talent can fix that.

Enboarder is an Australian company focused on improving the onboarding experience. We first heard about Enboarder after meeting their founder through a mutual friend. Impressed with their 21st-century approach to onboarding, we have stayed in touch and watched as the company expanded to service companies like McDonalds, Hugo Boss, and EA Games. The technology company uses emerging tech to lead new hires through a dynamic and personalized training experience through text messaging.

Although the organization has seen amazing results with their clients, not every client has had the same experience. Enboarder allows a company's human resources department to preload content that is delivered before the employee experiences his or her first day. For example, a new hire may get a preloaded text message from their "manager" asking, "What's your favorite food? That way, their manager can have it catered for them on their first day.

But there's a problem when the new hire finds that their manager is different in person. The technology made the employee feel valued, but the experience with the manager was anything but engaging. It was inauthentic. If the manager were genuinely involved in coaching their new hire, the technology would work brilliantly.

TECHNOLOGY IS NOT ADOPTED EQUALLY

There is a psychological phenomenon called reactance, which explains that people tend to resist change that is forced on them.[8] Have you ever adopted a new communication platform and only a handful of employees used it? Reactance takes hold because, as human beings, we don't like the feeling of having our choices taken away. Or worse, we don't like it when someone else's choice is forced upon us.

There is another phenomenon at work. Technology can mimic progress. A new invoicing program takes time to implement. It requires attention, training, and experimentation. If not checked, the mere act of adopting the program can make the user feel like they are getting work done. In reality, they had not processed any more invoices than before they accessed the platform. Psychologists have determined we feel a rush of accomplishment when we buy a solution, so much so that it often delays action that will lead to results.[9]

TECHNOLOGY WON'T SAVE A BAD CULTURE

If downloading an app could make a difference, all of us would be richer, fitter, on time, and less stressed out. However, we all know that simply signing up for a course doesn't guarantee results. You must take action over time to turn that hope into a habit. Do you have a fitness tracker? You may think that it is helping you stay on top of your fitness goals, but research shows it may be making you fat.

One study called out "the dirty secret of wearables," citing that, "These devices fail to drive long-term sustained engagement for a majority of users." Endeavour Partners' research found that "...more than half of U.S. consumers who have owned an activity tracker no longer use it. A third of U.S. consumers who have owned one stopped using the device within six months of receiving it."[10] Why? Because technology provides information, but information without action is useless.

If technology alone can't fix our collective health, it certainly can't fix employee turnover. The issue of employee turnover is a human problem, not a technology problem. There is no learning management system or communications platform that the CHP executive could have used to speak with the repair tech like that. It required the reasonable judgment of a leader with high emotional intelligence.

Technology is a tool for getting things done, not a shortcut for leaders to avoid leading. Technology can either increase the effectiveness of great leadership or increase the damage of poor leadership. It's that simple. A leader that is intentional about seeing, growing, and involving his employees will become more productive with technology. A leader that isn't intentional about the use and application of technology will never keep them longer.

ESSENTIALS TO USING TECHNOLOGY

Better technology will not save you. Technology is an amplifier of what is already within your organization. Leaders who over-rely on technology will never experience different results. This myth is dangerous because merely using a program or downloading an app can give you the feeling of progress. However, a system will only work if it is implemented. You will only experience the results of the Keep Them Longer method when you commit to bringing transformation first. Technology can scale transformation, but will only be successful when the leader is first transformed.

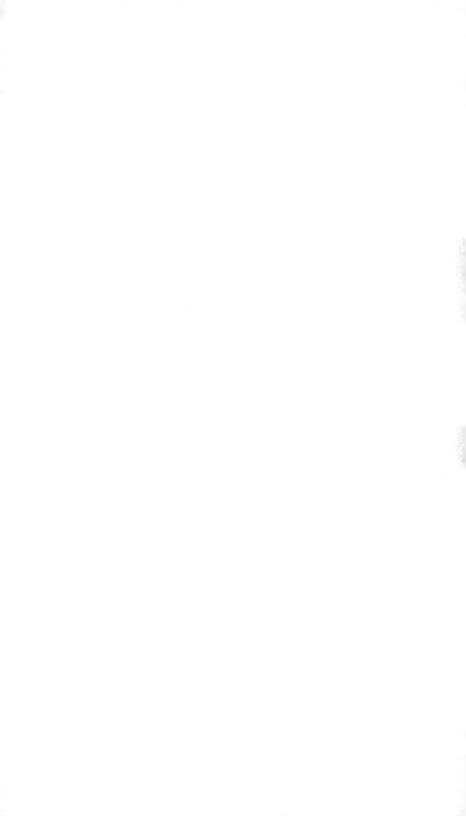

6

LIE #3
"Let's Tackle
One Thing at
a Time."

"Apple is executing wonderfully on many of the wrong things."[1] –Steve Jobs, Co-founder of Apple

On the night of April 20, 2010, an oil rig named Deepwater Horizon exploded in the Gulf of Mexico. High-pressure methane gas had expanded into the drilling riser and eventually made its way into the drilling rig where it ignited and exploded, engulfing the entire platform.[2]

John Bettencourt was the second helicopter pilot to arrive on the scene. John is in his mid-forties now, tall with chocolate brown hair that he boyishly brushes towards the front. He loves talking about growing up in the Northern California country and his experience in ROTC, where he learned about hard work, honesty, and starching his clothes. It was months after meeting him that we discovered his role in the famous event turned Hollywood blockbuster movie, which makes sense. John's calmness could be misinterpreted as shyness. But that would be wrong. He's quick to admit faults, and he's the kind of guy that shows up five minutes before your scheduled meetings. John is the kind of leader you want in charge.

John was an instructor pilot in the Coast Guard. He was stationed at what they call "The Schoolhouse" in Mobile, Alabama. On the evening of the explosion, John and his co-pilot, Dan Howe, had just finished a 10-hour workday where the two had been out training. John was wrapping up the paperwork in the office for his last flight when Dan took a call that would change their lives. There were 126 crew members on an inflamed oil rig that needed rescuing.

Dan left the office to assemble a crew. John immediately began executing a new flight plan. As the helicopter took off from the sleepy Alabama base and started toward the water, they could see the 300-foot flames burning on the Horizon at 150 miles out. When they arrived on the scene, the crew immediately began assessing the situation. Could they see men in the water? What was the visibility through the smoke and flames? What role did the other aircraft play in the operation?

There was an airplane that took command 2,000 feet above the scene. But it wasn't long until communication was scarce and unreliable from the command above. As they flew with the door open, the crew could feel the heat of the flames. Unsure whether or not there would be a second explosion, John and Dan decided to continue their rescue efforts.

The swimmers had been deployed and went below to begin extracting patients. As they went to pick up their rescue swimmer, John recalls looking down and seeing him slipping around on the oil-covered deck. As the pilot in command, John was trying to convince himself that the scene wasn't that bad.

He could see men still in the water, and he knew that they would be extracting survivors out one-by-one. But he never knew the gravity of the situation until the rescue swimmer returned. What the swimmer had seen was vastly different than what John was experiencing from the air. He saw men badly burned all over their bodies, workers with significant head injuries, screams and yelling, smoke, and the smell of burning oil and flesh.

Eventually, it was 5 a.m., and they had been searching for survivors for seven hours. John communicated to the command plane that they needed to be cycled out to refuel. No response. Another communication was dispatched to the command plane and still no answer to the request to cycle out. There were two options. Wait for consensus from command and risk the survival of his crew or take the necessary action. The stakes were too high and the problem so serious that John could not afford to do just one thing at a time. John decided to protect his team and his rescued patients and seek fuel. They had to take ownership of the event and not wait for the command overhead to lead their operation.

When you are hundreds of miles offshore, the only refueling option is landing on an oil rig. They set out towards another rig to refuel their quickly diminishing tank. What they found was another aircraft on the helipad and communication tower shut down. They went to another rig nearby. There was an aircraft on that helipad actively refueling.

As John looked down at his empty gas tank indicator, he made a decision. He would have no option but to land in the water. John couldn't help but think about how the news headlines would read the next day. Putting the chopper down in the water was something that they had trained for, but nothing that he would elect for his crew. Immediately after determining that a water landing was their only option, John was interrupted by Dan.

"We're good to land!"

While John had accepted the fate of a worst-case scenario, his co-pilot had been calling down to the rig and was able to get the other aircraft moved. If both pilots had only prepared for one outcome, their safety and survival would have been compromised. But both John and Dan were trained to tackle multiple problems from multiple angles. Never just one.

As the sun came up, John and his crew made their way home with a full tank of gas and a stunned sense of survival. John and his team were awarded Air Medals, one of the highest honors you can receive in military aviation. The explosion was the largest marine oil spill in the history of the petroleum industry, with 210 million gallons of oil spilling into the Gulf of Mexico.[3] Most leaders do the right things in the wrong order at the wrong time.

The best leaders do the right things in the right order at the right time—just like John.

DO YOU WANT IT BAD ENOUGH TO DO SOMETHING?

You have great talent. At least, that's what you thought when you hired them. They were competent. They had the right skill sets. They went to reputable schools and had relevant experience in your industry. They even interviewed well. But things have changed. Their drive is gone, and so is your excitement.

Leaders scratch their heads thinking about what happened between their employees' first day and their last—and why that timeline seems to be getting shorter. We have worked with hundreds of companies on their employee retention solutions and have seen incredible million-dollar cost savings. As a result, we have discovered that there are two types of companies who talk about retention.

The first type doesn't know they have a retention problem. Managers complain about losing people. The human resources department scrambles to find replacements. But these companies never take the time to reflect on the cause or cost of this turnover. Asking one of their executives about their retention becomes a short and often uninformed conversation. For these companies, ignorance is bliss—until it's too late.

The second type of company recognizes that they have a problem keeping their people and understand that it will require swift action to fix it. They take a measured but realistic view to increase engagement and reduce turnover. But then, when it's time to implement the solution, there's always a moment of hesitation.

"I know we need to do this, but we have to do this other thing first because we've already started," they say. "We absolutely must take steps to cut our turnover, but we just got a new learning management system. We have to train our people on that first." Or we hear this other well-worn excuse: "This is a priority, but we

need to push it until next fiscal year so we can better focus on it."
Right.

The shorter version of this is, "Your solution for reducing
churn is exactly right, but it's not enough of a priority for us to stop
doing what we want right now." Which company are you? Do your
leaders see the problem or ignore the issue? Do you take action or
delay results?

To us, the hesitation is no surprise. If your company is losing
talent at an alarming rate, the solution is going to feel different
than the problem. It's going to be uncomfortable. It will require a
different mindset. It's going to mean swallowing pride, admitting
mistakes to re-establish trust, and leading with a humble and
helping heart. No one willingly elects to do that which is
uncomfortable.

However, the uncomfortable makes way for the extraordinary.

THE SECRET TO BREAKING BAD HABITS
WITHIN ORGANIZATIONS

Brain scientists can dissect a human brain and show precisely
where neural pathways have been "burned" into the brain from
repetitious activity.[4] When you first started tying your shoes, it
took effort. You had to think about putting one lace around the
other and pulling it through. You had to consider how long the
laces were so you wouldn't trip over them. You were careful to
pull tight, or the laces would annoyingly untie throughout the day.

The first ten times that you tied your shoes, you were accessing the prefrontal cortex, the thinking brain.[5] This part of the brain is where you process new information. When the action is done enough, it makes its way to the back of your brain, the basal ganglia. This is the part of the brain that does things on automatic for you.[6] Imagine if you still had to think that hard to tie your shoes this morning!

When a change is introduced to the brain, red flags go up. Your prefrontal cortex goes into overdrive. From an evolutionary standpoint, our minds cannot tell the difference between positive change (the climate changing to be more bearable for human life) or negative change (a new predator or disease).[7] Both require an immense amount of energy, which is why we avoid making changes in our life.

When we are first born, our minds are malleable, open to change, and eager to learn. As we age, our brain creates rules based on experience (e.g., "The stove is hot. Don't touch."). These rules help us avoid relearning the same lessons over and over again. But it can also lead to negative behaviors and bad habits. Modern organizations work much as the brain does.

When we introduce new concepts and they get rejected, our organizational brain stores that as data for future use. If it happens enough, you begin to see a rule forming, and you never introduce a new concept again. When a new program rolls out that is overly complicated and poorly executed, our organizational brain stores that, too. So when someone suggests a sweeping change, the organization's memory kicks in and reminds everyone that big is bad. This response happens even when the solution is desperately needed and nothing like the previous failed attempts.

SO, WHAT'S YOUR "BEST WORST EXCUSE"?

How does change happen? It takes full force effort. When leaders say, "I can't do one more thing," they are really saying something else. We have created a decoder to determine what someone is really saying when they are faking focus:

- "I don't have the capacity."
- "I can't possibly handle one more thing."
- "It's not a priority."
- "I don't really know how to do it."
- "I'm going to do the thing that I already started."
- "We're too far into this."
- "I know, but …"

These excuses are an issue because problems don't get solved in places of comfort; they get resolved in places of discomfort. Solving problems requires that we break old mindsets, change goals, and execute on new tasks. The breaking, changing, and implementing dislodge us from our well-rehearsed mental habits. So when we hear, "You're right, but let's tackle one thing at a time," what's being said is, "I don't want to do this right now because it's uncomfortable."

We all want to be more focused. Countless books are authored on finding clarity, decluttering, and streamlining behavior. It's become a societal badge of honor to eliminate the unnecessary and elevate the singular. But despite our collective push towards single-tasking, we continue to get stuck.

"Let's tackle one thing at a time," is the most dangerous of excuses because it sounds responsible. It makes the leader appear prudent, measured, and strategic. But it never challenges the leader to ask if they are addressing the right problem and applying the right solution.

GREAT LEADERS COMPOUND, THEY DON'T MULTI-TASK

Albert Einstein stated, "[Compounding] is the greatest mathematical discovery of all time."[8]

Now there's nothing wrong with handling one major issue at a time. Multi-tasking has been proven by brain science to be impossible.[9] We certainly aren't advocating for taking your company in multiple directions simultaneously. No organization could survive very long if every initiative received equal attention or funding. Tackling the wrong thing with singular focus continues to hamstring your results because it feels like progress.

What's important is the sequence. In what order are you handling your organization's problems? If you've got a significant turnover issue, then training your people on the new learning management system isn't going to cut your turnover. It might feel good to do so, but it isn't going to lead to results. It's like checking off an item on your "To-Do" list that never needed to be on the list in the first place. We already know that technology can't change hearts and minds. Only leaders can change hearts and minds—and they do so by seeing, growing, and involving their talent every day.

Turnover is not about handling "one thing at a time." It's about managing "the right thing at the right time." That is the essence of compounding. It allows the momentum experienced in one area to lift other areas.

Steve Jobs understood this principle. Jobs, of course, was one of the founders of Apple. Apple is one of the world's most recognizable brands and the first company to ever hit a $1 trillion market capitalization.[10] Pretty impressive. Despite being one of the founders, Jobs was ousted from Apple in 1985 after a scuffle over product focus with then CEO, John Sculley. After leaving, Jobs went on to start two other companies, one of them being Pixar.[11]

He spent over a decade in exile from Apple until 1996 when he returned as interim CEO. By then, Apple was losing money and slamming through CEOs. The final quarter before Jobs's return, Apple's sales plummeted by 30 percent.

It was so bad that Dell founder, Michael Dell, said that if he were in charge, he would "shut it down and give the money back to the shareholders."[12] The outlook for Apple was bleak. After taking over as interim CEO, Jobs used the 1997 Macworld Conference to chart a new path for the company. He talked about making changes to the board, its product focus, and partnerships.[13]

But there was one thing that Jobs said that made all the difference. He said, "Apple is executing wonderfully on many of the wrong things."[14] You read that right. The most profound thing in his speech was, "Apple is executing wonderfully on many of the wrong things." In getting reacquainted to the company and preparing for his speech, Jobs discovered that Apple had very talented people. But, they were not executing on the right priorities. It was going to take more than changing one thing at a time to save Apple. It would take a targeted but comprehensive approach to leadership, development, growth, and innovation.

Jobs immediately launched a multi-faceted approach to saving the company. This approach included a partnership with Microsoft that injected $150 million into Apple, cutting the product line by 70 percent, and reducing the workforce by about 3,000 employees.[15]

"Deciding what not to do is as important as deciding what to do," Jobs said in his autobiography. Further, he said, "It's true for companies, and it's true for products."[16]

Jobs's approach to tackling the right things at the right time was complemented by his signature "question everything" demeanor. His comprehensive approach to saving the company paid off. The first fiscal year after his return, Apple lost $1.04 billion. One year later, the company turned a $309 million profit.[17]

That's doing the right things in the right order at the right time.

ESSENTIALS TO TACKLING MORE THAN ONE THING AT A TIME

Multi-tasking is a dirty word in leadership circles. We elevate singular focus and laser-sharp attention over comprehensive solutions. Although there is power in focus, too many leaders use single-tasking as an excuse not to prioritize what is most important. Great leaders determine what the real problem is and situate their organization to address the most critical problems first. Don't try to fix every problem in your organization at once. Focus on solving the right problems at the right time in the right order.

7

LIE #4
**"We Need
More Buy-In."**

"If the discovery is yours, the duty is yours."

You don't need to wait until others see the problem. By then, it will be too late. Allyn Pierce told *The Washington Post* that his white Toyota Tundra was his "dream truck."[1] He had spent long weekends modifying the four-wheel-drive monster, adding a lift kit, new suspension, grill, and utility rack over the truck bed.

The truck got its nickname, "The Pandra," from three metal plates intentionally welded onto the roof rack. The plates formed the face of a panda. Allyn never knew that his "dream truck" would one day serve a purpose. That day came.

In 2018, California experienced one of the most destructive wildfires in its history. The "Camp Fire," as it was called, was also the deadliest wildfire in the United States since 1918. It took place in Butte County, California. Eighty-five people died, and nearly 19,000 buildings collapsed or burned. The estimated damage was $16.5 billion.[2]

Amid the tragedy rose a hero who didn't want to be known as one. Allyn Pierce was more than a truck enthusiast. He was a registered nurse and an intensive care unit (ICU) manager at Adventist Health Feather River Hospital. On November 8, 2018, he showed up to work before 8 a.m. Around that time, the Camp Fire was threatening his hospital. Allyn and his colleagues worked quickly to evacuate dozens of patients by loading them into ambulances.

By 9:30 a.m., Allyn discovered something. He and his colleagues were among the last to evacuate. So he had them jump into The Pandra (also on Instagram: @The_Pandra). Heading down Pierson Road in the town of Paradise, California, they got stuck in a line of cars with flames roaring on either side of the road.

They couldn't escape, as there was an abandoned truck burning to the left. On the right, there was the faint outline of a fire engine. Allyn explained the firefighters had put up mylar blankets in the windows of the fire engine to protect themselves from the heat. Allyn's colleagues quickly got out of his truck and took refuge with the firefighters.

He stayed in The Pandra alone. In his interview, he said he could hear propane tanks exploding in the distance. He recorded a "goodbye" video on his phone for his family. Nowhere to go, he waited as the flames kissed the side of his truck. That was, until a bulldozer knocked the flaming truck to his left out of the way. Seeing his opening, he turned around and raced back to the hospital where he discovered emergency personnel tending to newly arrived patients.

Working with the emergency crews, he jumped in. He went into the hospital, gathered supplies, and set up a triage area in the parking lot. As the fire closed in on the hospital, they moved their makeshift emergency room to the helipad. At around 2 p.m. everyone was able to evacuate safely after firefighters said the road was clear.

Soon after, Allyn was reunited with his family. Reflecting on the situation, he told *The Post*, "Everyone worked together...It was a complete lack of ego. There was never an argument."[3] And there was something else. When it was all over, The Pandra had gotten its panda spots. The sides of the bright white truck had been charred like a toasted marshmallow, leaving dark black spots all around the vehicle. The red brake lights that were once bold and bright were melted away like wax. The bumpers all around the truck were mangled and bent from pushing past abandoned vehicles and through the high brush.

But it didn't matter. The truck had served its purpose. When Toyota found out about Allyn's bravery, they were so impressed that they sent him a brand new, bright white Toyota Tundra.[4] Then, a custom paint shop gave the new truck panda spots as well. For Allyn, it was simple. When he saw those in need of help, he helped them—with no hesitation.

Therein lies the principle: "If the discovery is yours, the duty is yours."

DEATH BY CORPORATE BUZZWORD

If we were to create a corporate index of buzzwords and phrases that people say in meetings, the phrase "We need more buy-in" would be one of them. Here's what happens. A leader discovers that they've lost their top five performers in the last three months. So they convene a meeting (or five) to talk about the issue and craft a solution. Then their colleagues chime in. "We've got to get John on board, or this won't go anywhere…Sally isn't going to like this, so our hands are tied…We don't have a budget, so we can't make changes right now."

Then the leader who discovered the problem concludes, "We can't do anything until we get more buy-in." And then nothing happens. Don't get us wrong. Generating buy-in is key to getting things done as a team. It's dangerous to make a decision that affects the entire group without consulting each person.

But buy-in is not required for individual action. Buy-in is not necessary for leaders to change the way they lead. Buy-in is not required to see, grow, and involve your people. There is a difference between generating buy-in and putting off what needs to be done today. Waiting for buy-in is the most dangerous of the myths. It feels prudent. It feels like action without actually making a decision. It feels good to address a problem and then defer to others or a later date. It makes you look like a quality leader who cares about the input of your people.

What most leaders don't understand is that they're waiting for buy-in, but their people are waiting for them.

Allyn understood this principle. Rather than wait for others to agree to help, he took action. He didn't run over to the firefighters and ask their permission to help. He didn't wait for someone to designate him the "Captain of Search and Rescue." There were no business cards or nameplates involved. Allyn did what needed to be done.

It may not be life or death for you like it was for Allyn, but turnover is directly related to the survival of your company. We understand that you aren't working a deadly forest fire. You work in an office with ever-moving deadlines, annoying coworkers, and mind-numbing commutes. But there are social norms that have crept into the way we live, work, and communicate. Walk up to a door at the same time as another person. Odds are you will be engaged in a "nice-off"—a socially acceptable banter of "No, you go" and "No, really, I insist, you were here first." Individuals who take the initiative without the consent of the team are considered pushy, bossy, and unlikable.

Whether we're in the contracting phase or working with a client, we hear the "buy-in" excuse a lot. More often than not, it is a veiled excuse for not taking individual action towards solving critical people problems.

Let me tell you about one of our favorite "if only" moments. We call them "if only" because we were so close to getting the deal, but one little thing—or, should we say, person—held it up. We were introduced to a large international organization that certifies industry professionals. We met with the executive team to discuss how Millennials are shaping the future of membership organizations and how we could help them become a more youthful organization.

When meeting day rolled around, ten or so executives and support staff splayed across a large well-lit but typical conference room outside of Washington, D.C. The meeting was running as meetings do. There were introductions, probing questions as to who we were and what we did, sharing of data and anecdotes, and then a wrap-up discussion of next steps. Their needs were real. Our solutions were clear. There was consensus in the room that a proposal would be appropriate. As we were leaving, the executive director shook our hands and stated in a promising tone, "We look forward to working with you guys. It's clear you know your stuff and can help us out."

So how did a successful meeting that should have been a slam dunk turn into one of the longest string-alongs in our company history?

What the leaders in the room had failed to mention was that they had just hired a new special programs associate who would be handling their youth outreach. This young woman was on a mission to make her mark. The leaders didn't want to step on the toes of their newest team member. In an attempt to respect her role and responsibilities, they tasked her to work directly with us on the proposal—lucky us.

They wanted her buy-in before moving forward.

It started as a clean solution to their immediate needs. It turned into a sprawling scope of work that seemed more concerned with her agenda than the corporate goals stated by the executive director. She did not share the vision of the leadership nor understand the importance of the mission. She was being asked to care about something she did not believe in. The countless emails, corrections, clarifications, and phone calls to appease her requests came to a sudden end when we decided to terminate the proposal.

Unfortunately, the opportunity to work with the organization never materialized because of well-intentioned leadership focused on "buy-in." Three years later, the organization still has no Millennial outreach or retention strategy and is one of the thousands of groups struggling to grow their membership base.

IF YOU'RE WAITING FOR UNIVERSAL BUY-IN, YOU'LL NEVER GET IT

Do you have someone in your life who hates change? They were the last ones to get a smartphone. They are wary of new ways of doing things. They question why their GPS app insists on going another way to the airport. They are late adopters. We know them. We love them. We are frustrated by them.

The "Diffusion of Innovation Theory" is a well-understood principle within marketing. But it also guides how new ideas get spread and implemented within an organization. Five groups are described in the Diffusion of Innovation Theory.[5]

1. Innovators

The first group is the innovators.[6] They love change so much that when change isn't happening, they create it. They are entrepreneurs, inventors, poets, and creatives. Innovators see the world differently.

They do not consider the downside of a new idea but see what the world would look like as if their dream already existed. Our society heroizes these individuals after their inventions become widely recognized as useful. They are the Steve Jobses, Thomas Edisons, and Sara Blakelys of the world.

But they are also the individuals in organizations who are questioning the status quo and developing new ways of doing things. They are shaking things up and frustrating the system. Innovators can be challenging to work with and work for. Once they have an idea about how things should change, they are stubbornly committed to effecting that change at all costs.

2. The Early Adopters

Unlike the Innovators, Early Adopters advocate for the invention rather than create it.[7] They are the first to buy the newest technology and instantly become brand ambassadors for their favorite gizmos. Similar to Innovators, Early Adopters love and appreciate new ideas and seek out opportunities to learn or be challenged.

These are the individuals you work with that get excited for positive change within the organization and readily share their ideas and thoughts on how they can help. They attend brainstorming meetings, research best practices, and help recruit others to join the team.

3. The Early Majority

Once the Early Adopters normalize and systemize a new way of doing things, the Early Majority comes along and adopts it as well.[8] At first, they're hesitant to put their social capital on the line to advocate for something that may or may not work. However, once they come on board, they also become brand ambassadors for the change. Some Early Majority adopters in organizations only join because they don't want to be left behind. Others participate because their doubts or fears have been eased. Some join simply because they find the change useful or healthy.

The Early Majority will support the new program or way of doing things, but they may not always advocate for it. They are the individuals in a company who need more information and more persuading, but will eventually do what is best for the group.

4. The Late Adopters

Late Adopters are the most skeptical group.[9] They will eventually get on board, but only after some time has passed. They have questions from the beginning. They challenge the need for change. They question the credentials of the Innovators and the wisdom of the Early Adopters. The Late Adopters are the next wave of the majority.

The Late Adopters in a company come along but with feet dragging and want the world to know that they still don't think it is a good idea. They readily share their concerns about how things are being done, what other priorities are being implemented, and reserve the right to say, "I told you so."

5. The Laggards

The Laggards never adopt the change.[10] If they can, they will stand in the way of change happening at all. The Laggards cannot be convinced that the change is necessary. Most laggards believe any change is harmful and cannot be convinced with science, data, or personal experience. These types will either not go along with the change or quit because the change shifts their sense of security.

Understanding this paradigm is the key to breaking the excuse of buy-in inside your organization. Even the most groundbreaking solution will go ignored if the proposal is handed to a late adopter when it should be given to the Innovators and Early Adopters. It is useless to delay action until you receive universal buy-in. Some will adopt it freely, others will adopt it slowly, and still others will never adopt it at all. So don't wait.

THE THREE PRIMARY "BUY-IN" EXCUSES

When leaders say they need more buy-in, they are articulating one of three excuses:

1. "I don't have the authority or influence to make the necessary change."

The ultimate question is not about authority but one of responsibility. Shared vision creates an environment where big goals are achieved. But it is still dependent upon the intentional action of every individual on the team. Leadership titan John Maxwell defines leadership as influence.[11] We all have someone or something that we are influencing. So who's inside your sphere of influence?

We have a friend with three children under the age of 10. She mentioned to us that she feels entirely out of control most days. Her weekends are spent shuttling them from friends' houses to ballet and soccer practice. "It's like they're running my life. I can't even take a shower without one of them yelling for me from the other room. I can't wait for them to get older so that the oldest can help take care of the other ones."

To the outside world, the children were running her life. But what our friend had failed to realize was that she is letting them. She has complete influence over those little humans. She is their leader. She was waiting for backup from one of the kids she was parenting. She was making a mistake most business leaders make today. They are deferring the influence they have today because they are hopeful that someone else will come in and fix the problem for them.

We helped her define the areas of her life in which she felt the most out of control. We then developed a plan for how she could make definitive changes that would help her feel more rested and her children become more autonomous. Our friend began to witness her children become more self-controlled and independent. She started to utilize the incredible influence she already had.

2. "I am unsure if this will work. If I get more people to agree, it spreads the risk."

In the second half of the 20th century, Edward Banfield was an important name to know. The American political scientist advised Richard Nixon, Gerald Ford, and Ronald Reagan. Edward's legacy goes beyond simple campaigning. His insight into how politicians interact with constituents has shaped the way we view leadership. Richard Banfield was the first to coin the term "political capital" in 1961. In his book, Political Influence, Banfield described political capital as a "stock of influence." A politician must spend or save this influence wisely or face being kicked by those that once elected him.[12]

The same is true in business. Individuals at every level of an organization measure the type and frequency of risk they introduce. We often hear about big rewards coming only after big risks. Marissa Mayer is the President and CEO of Yahoo! She said:

"I always did something I was a little not ready to do. I think that's how you grow. When there's that moment of 'Wow, I'm not really sure I can do this,' and you push through those moments, that's when you have a breakthrough."[13]

Indecision is often the result of fear—fear of backlash, poor results, and of it hurting your ability to get a raise or promotion. But there's something else. You may be avoiding change because you are looking for a complete program. You want someone to give you a blueprint for you to take and use because that feels less risky.

People want a program because it gives them finality. It gives them the certainty that there is a path forward. There's nothing wrong with that. That is why we provide full programs for human resources departments and management teams that cut turnover. However, we don't build programs for the program's sake. For us, it's always about the principles before we build the program. Installing a new program takes time. It takes attention. It takes action. Although we believe in the power of process, no plan will work unless you work first.

3. "I don't want to make a decision on this right now."

Life feels overwhelming for most Americans. Seventy-nine percent of Americans feel frequent stress in their daily lives.[14] Making one more decision can feel like an enormous task—especially if there is uncertainty in one or more areas of your life. The Cheshire Cat in Alice in Wonderland reminds us that indecision is still a decision.

When Alice asked, "What road do I take?"

The Cheshire cat asked, "Where do you want to go?"

"I don't know," Alice answered.

"Then," said the cat, "it doesn't matter."[15]

What's worse is that we praise people who defer big decisions. We consider them contemplative, wise, and responsible. All decisions should be given the appropriate amount of reflection. But imagine what the world would look like if the most significant decisions took the longest time to figure out. Wars would never end as leaders quarreled. Surgeries would last for weeks as surgeons consulted and deferred to one another. Couples would never get married for fear of choosing the wrong person.

We understand that big decisions must be made in high-pressure scenarios, even if all of the information is not present. So why do we delay making a decision in situations that are not life or death and then praise ourselves for our wisdom and prudence? There are numerous books on making effective and efficient decisions.

The summarizing principle is this: If you wait too long to make a decision, the decision will be made without you—and you won't necessarily like the result. Ultimately, the responsibility to lead and influence your team is yours. It is not the executive team's responsibility nor the responsibility of another department. It is not even your employees' responsibility (more on that in the next chapter).

ESSENTIALS TO GETTING BUY-IN

If the discovery is yours, the duty is yours. Important changes often get overlooked or delayed because the leader wants to defer their decision-making to someone else. They seek acceptance so badly that they are willing to wait indefinitely to get everyone on board. This will never happen. Every person on the team has varying levels of comfort when it comes to change. If you project an "early adopter" characteristic on someone who is a "later adopter," you will both come out frustrated. Leaders who wait for others to make the decisions are not true leaders. True leaders influence others, no matter their formal authority or position. They take responsibility where appropriate and take action to create positive change.

8

LIE #5
"When Does it Become Their Responsibility?"

It's pretty funny, isn't it, how yawning is contagious?

You've seen it before. You're in a classroom or conference room and someone yawns. Then, without having the slightest hint of fatigue, you find yourself yawning along. It is a fascinating phenomenon that's been the subject of much curiosity and scientific study. Experts have even studied whether contagious yawning is linked to empathy, emotional intelligence, autism, and age.[1]

While the evidence is hardly conclusive as to those links, science has concluded that, yes, yawning is socially contagious.[2] Not just in humans. Yawning also looks to be contagious among chimpanzees, baboons, dogs, and possibly sheep. Yawning is contagious between humans and dogs (more so if the human is the owner of the dog).[3] Whether contagious yawning stems from empathy or something else, perhaps it is this simple: If someone else yawns, you're more likely to yawn, too.

Beyond yawning, there's something else that's socially contagious and harmful to an organization's culture: blaming others.

In 2009, Dr. Nathaneal Fast, Associate Professor of Management at the University of Southern California's Marshall School of Business, and Dr. Lara Tiedens, former Associate Dean at Stanford and now President of Scripps college, discovered that blaming others is socially contagious. It can be caught like a cold virus and spread through society or the office. They dubbed it "Blame Contagion."[4] The first of its kind, the study measured whether or not people were more likely to blame others for their failures if they first saw someone else cast the blame.

The study's participants read a news piece about a prominent failure of then California Governor, Arnold Schwarzenegger. Governor Schwarzenegger was elected in a special election and was not as popular with the California legislature as he had been with the voters. To get his agenda passed, Governor Schwarzenegger had chosen to leverage a similar special election to get California citizens to support four of his executive propositions. It was a disaster. Californians shot down all of the Governor's propositions, and the special election cost the state, special interest groups, and voters more than $300 million.[5]

After reading the news clip, roughly half of the study's participants were shown a manufactured statement by Governor Schwarzenegger taking full responsibility for the failure. The other half were shown a manufactured statement by the Governor blaming special interest groups (which is what he did).[6]

Then the study takes a turn. The study's participants were then asked to consider a personal failure of their own and write it down. It could have been anything—a failed marriage, a poorly executed business plan, or a badly burnt lasagna. Then they were prompted to write down who or what was responsible for their failure. The results were astounding.

The participants exposed to Governor Schwarzenegger's blaming statement were more likely to attribute blame to something or someone else for their own failures. Those that reviewed the Governor taking full responsibility were less likely to blame others.[7] In other words, if someone else blames, you're more likely to blame, too.

In the context of the workplace, herein lies two principles:

1. Your Employees Will Mirror Your Actions.
2. You Must Be What You Want Them to Be.

In our work with top companies on keeping their talent longer, we talk to managers, directors, vice presidents, and CEOs who are exhausted. In their minds, they've done everything they can. "We've done engagement surveys. We've thrown big blowout holiday parties and employee barbeques costing us thousands of dollars," they say. But nothing gets better.

At the height of their exhaustion, they ask us, "When does it become their responsibility?" Translation: "I've done my part. Now it's on them, the employees." This question is classic blame-shifting, no different than the experiment's statement by Governor

Schwarzenegger blaming special interest groups for his special election failure.

When it comes to keeping talent longer, the responsibility (or blame) never shifts to the employees. If a company fails, it is the individuals at the top that are held responsible, not the people on the bottom. Leaders are always responsible for keeping their talent. Always. Amid this blame-shifting, some of the leaders we meet go as far as to say their employees "should be thankful even to have a job here." In other words, the employees should be on their knees, thanking God for the privilege of working at the company.

But should the company consider it a privilege to have employees, or should the employee consider it a privilege to have a job? On the surface, the answer is, "Both should consider it a privilege." But beneath the surface, it is the leaders who should consider it more of a privilege to have employees at all. Great leaders lead with gratefulness.

It is a company that has more to lose. If an employee loses his or her job, there's always another or, at worst, a social safety net. On the other hand, a company without employees isn't a company at all. So who should consider it more of a privilege? The company. Thus, a company and its leaders should avoid shifting the blame for its turnover woes to the employees.

IMPACT OF THE BLAME CONTAGION ON YOUR TEAM

The "blame game" becomes dangerous within an organization for three important reasons.

1. Blame Causes People to Not Take Responsibility for Themselves.

"Captain, the passengers are starting to make their way to the lifeboats by themselves."[8]

It was Friday, January 13, 2012 when the Costa Concordia was rounding its first few days of a seven-day journey through the Mediterranean. Passengers were becoming acquainted with all that the flagship vessel of the Costa fleet had to offer. They were exploring the ship's 13 decks. It had four swimming pools with twisting water slides, an outdoor movie pavilion, a two-story spa, casino, and seemingly endless dining options. The boat had everything a modern cruise liner could offer. The passengers had not yet been briefed on the safety procedures of the ship. That was scheduled for the next day.[9]

Couples were celebrating engagements. Families were relaxing on much-needed vacations. Retirees were checking off their bucket lists. While the passengers reveled in the novelty of the ship, the crew began their well-worn routine. The Costa Concordia crew was led by a seven-year veteran captain, Francisco Schettino.[10]

Captain Schettino was born in 1960 to an Italian naval family. After attending a nautical institute, he was hired by Costa Cruises as a security officer. It was not long before the ambitious young man became second-in-command. When the Costa Concordia was completed, Schettino became its captain.[11]

That evening, Captain Schettino instructed his crew to conduct a sail-by-salute. It was a standard operation that brought the ship close to shore to give the passengers a better view of the Mediterranean island of Giglia. Deck officers were in charge of the operation while the captain ate dinner. They needed to keep the ship away from the island shore and maintain 15 knots.[12] When a small outcropping of rocks blocked the ship's path, Schettino left his dinner and instructed the helmsman to steer the ship away from the outcropping. Schettino had been barking orders in his native Italian at the Indonesian helmsman. He spoke neither English nor Italian. When Schettino made the order, the helmsman did not understand and took the ship in the opposite direction of the captain's order—2,300 feet closer to shore than intended. Captain Schettino tried to correct the mistake, but it was already too late.[13]

At approximately 9:45 p.m., the Costa Concordia dragged across rocks off the Italian coast. Water rushed through the 174-foot portside gash, filling five compartments. Immediately the ship's electricity shut off and the emergency lighting came on. The engine room flooded, and the rudder lost mobility. The ship was now floating without direction with over 4,200 passengers and crew on board.[14] During the 19-month trial prosecuting Schettino, maritime experts noted the crash was unavoidable due to the coordinates originally placed in by Schettino.[15]

Now, large water vessels like the Costa Concordia are constructed in segments to prevent one blow from capsizing the entire ship. But because the gash spanned multiple compartments, the damage was too much to contain.

Announcements were made to calm worried passengers who were interrupted at their card tables, lounge chairs, and white tablecloth dinners. The crew assured passengers that everything was fine. When a panicked passenger called her daughter in Italy, the concerned daughter alerted the Italian Coast Guard.

The Italian Coast Guard immediately called the command tower on the Concordia to see what was going on. The command tower informed the Coast Guard that they were merely experiencing a blackout. But the head engineer had just been to the bridge to tell Captain Schettino, and his officers, that another three compartments had flooded and the ship was beginning to list.[16]

On their own, the passengers began making their way to level four where the lifeboats were stored. Constant cries from the loudspeaker assured them, "The situation is under control." Panicked smartphone footage can still be found online as a 21st century Titanic began to manifest. Passengers worked together in teams to quickly and unskillfully lower the lifeboats into the water.[17]

It was nearly an hour after the crash that the first rescue vessel arrived. At this point, the ship was at a 25-degree angle. The lifeboats were being filled and deployed at a rapid pace. Captain Schettino finally announced an abandon ship and immediately went to the fourth deck to board a rescue boat himself. His fellow officers followed suit, and soon, the command deck was completely abandoned. It was every man and woman for themselves. The Captain was leaving the ship, and there were still passengers on board.[18]

Recordings of Schettino arguing with an Italian Coast Guard official about returning to the ship were later released across international news agencies. The Coast Guard was demanding that he return to the vessel and determine how many people were still on the boat. He never did. In his trial, Schettino would later claim that he tripped on the deck because of the ship's angle and "fell" into one of the lifeboats.[19] It turns out that he was neither a good captain nor a good liar.

Schettino also insisted on recorded calls that he was coordinating rescue efforts from his lifeboat. "What are you coordinating from there? Go on board!" the Coast Guard officer demanded. "Look, Schettino. You may have saved yourself from the sea. I am going to make sure you get in trouble. I am going to make you pay for this," the officer threatened.[20]

After long pauses and inaudible responses, Schettino eventually gave the Coast Guard a multi-part excuse for why he could not return to check for survivors. Their lifeboat stalled. It was too dark and he couldn't see anything on board. Meanwhile, 300 people were still on the ship.

At this point, the ship was on its side and resting on the rocks. The starboard side was completely submerged. Those left on the boat clung to the port side of the 952-foot-long cruise liner. They escaped by crawling across what was the bottom of the ship holding onto a small rope. The lifeboats spilled onto the shores of Giglio as the people of the island met them with blankets and food. The locals even welcomed survivors into their homes.[21]

The next morning, the Mediterranean sun rose and soon exposed the full extent of the tragedy. The Costa Concordia, a floating city the length of three football fields, was half-submerged just off the coast of the small Italian island.

Divers rescued an additional three survivors the next morning. Tragically, 32 people died in the Costa Concordia incident, most of whom were found in elevators making their way to the lifeboat deck.[22] The aftermath of the Costa Concordia tragedy resulted in a more than $2 billion salvage operation.[23] The Italian Coast Guard official who threatened Captain Schettino made good on his promise. Four crew members and one agent of the Costa Concordia Command Center were prosecuted and sentenced to roughly two years in prison.

Captain Schettino received the fate he deserved. After a rejected plea deal, Captain Schettino was handed a 16-year jail sentence for manslaughter, causing the wreck, and abandoning ship. Even after his conviction, he continued to claim no responsibility.[24] Later, analysts determined that if they had begun evacuating everyone after the impact was correctly diagnosed, they would have had all passengers off in 35 minutes. One hundred years after the Titanic, human error and arrogance yet again brought down a vessel that was considered unsinkable.

George Washington Carver is famed to have said, "Ninety-nine percent of the failures come from people who have the habit of making excuses."[25]

Accounts of the Costa Concordia show that Schettino was emotionally absent and distracted while captaining the ship, having brought along his mistress to join him in the Captain's quarters.[26] Distracted, he was not able to think and act appropriately. Schettino could have had a Captain Sully moment, but he chose the path of least resistance. He decided to let his poor daily habits dictate his breakout moments.

We read stories like these and assume that we would never be so selfish. However, leaders choose to point the finger at their employees every day. It was their fault the shipment was late. It was the responsibility of their staff to check the proposal for typing errors. It was the sales department's fault that they over-promised a timeline and now the customer is screaming over the phone. Is the employee responsible? Always. But an employee who does not see responsibility modeled will never take responsibility for themselves.

Taking responsibility, like anything else, is a matter of habit.

2. Blame Causes People to Be Less Innovative.

The question "When does it become their responsibility?" will not create the culture you need or want. Dr. Fast, reflecting on their "Blame Contagion" experiment, explains that laying blame makes the situation worse. In an interview with the University of Southern California News, he said, "Blame creates a culture of fear." If an employee sees a leader casting blame on others, they will be fearful of being blamed for something, become less willing to take risks, be less innovative or creative, and less likely to learn from their mistakes.[27]

There are two different types of conformity in adults. The first, informative influence, isn't helpful for this discussion. But the second is normative influence. This type of influence comes from the double-edged need to avoid rejection and find belonging. Normative influence happens when you take off your shoes at your friends' home without prompting because you see a pile of shoes by the front door. It occurs when you go to a meeting where everyone has their phone on the table, so you unconsciously do the same. But it also happens when you stop introducing new ideas because the group doesn't accept them.[28]

You are either being influenced by someone else's status quo or creating the status quo for others.

Let's say that you just got hired and are excited about your new role. It's a big step up for you in your career, and you have a lot of ideas about how you can help. Your brain can't stop thinking about how you can improve output, fix problems, and make a difference for the company. In essence, you are taking full responsibility for your role. After a few months on the job, you notice that your coworkers don't have the same tenacity as you. They begin to question the ideas you bring up in meetings. Your colleagues smile blankly when you suggest how a process can be improved and move on to the next subject as if you hadn't said anything. They only seem to care about getting their work done and getting out of the office by 5:30 p.m.

But you're still committed to doing a great job. You stay late after everyone leaves to get your work done ahead of schedule. You even come up with a new protocol within your department that is going over well. Everything is going great for you until the big boss catches wind that a group of employees isn't doing it his way. In the next department meeting, your approach is reprimanded in front of the entire group. You look over at your team whose heads are starting to hang lower and lower. You feel your face turn red from embarrassment. After the meeting, you recollect your thoughts and determine you will never feel this way again.

Blame is why most organizations lack motivation among their employees. The first six months of an employee's career includes excitement, innovation, and ownership. Then, slowly, reality sets in. No one seems to care about the role as much as they do. They see creative solutions being ignored or mocked and experimentation punished. That once-motivated employee now becomes a disengaged one.

3. Blame Causes Low Trust Among the Team.

What if we told you gossip is good?

That's what some researchers are arguing. Reading the research of University of Queensland's Dr. Roy Baumeister and his colleagues, there are two types of gossip: awe and shame. They say:

"In our view, gossip is a potentially powerful and efficient means of transmitting information about the rules, norms, and other guidelines for living in a culture."[29]

Awe gossip compliments a person in some way. "Did you hear how much money John is making at his new job?" or "I can't believe how generous your grandparents were with their wedding gift." Awe gossip is very different than shame gossip. "I can't believe she got pregnant so soon," or "I heard that Jack was out last week because he was in rehab."

We know that awe is more admirable than shame. What we don't realize is that shame gossip has its place, according to Dr. Baumesiter and his colleagues' work.[30] They argue that shame gossip, although potentially harmful to the individual, is suitable for society because it shows us what is unacceptable behavior. In truth, gossip informally regulates individual expression.

A new group member quickly learns what is acceptable and appropriate based on not just what the group praises, but on what the group mocks. It certainly feels good to be amongst one of the insiders who share the experiences, thoughts, and opinions of others. Humans are social creatures, and we continuously long for community and acceptance. However, our need to belong can be taken to such a degree that it creates a culture of fear and anxiety.[31]

Whether consciously or not, a culture ridden with gossip keeps individuals in line because the members do not want to be the object of their peers' criticism. They will dampen their work effort, change the way they dress or eat, or even adjust their expectations—all for the alluring sentiment of belonging. Healthy cultures spread positive rumors. Unhealthy organizations are ridden with ugly rumors.

Good parents teach their kids to avoid friendships with people who gossip. That makes sense. If they talk about someone else like that, you know they will be gossiping about you in no time. In fact, they probably already are. In the same way, when we coach companies on hiring, we encourage managers to listen to how candidates talk about past jobs. Are they grateful, frustrated, hurt, or feel used? All of these sentiments will come out when you ask the right questions. It is essential to listen to their responses. What they say about a past employer is what they will say about you.

When Captain Schettino abandoned the sinking Costa Concordia, he set a precedent amongst his crew. He taught without words that it was acceptable to put yourself above the passengers. Therefore, it is no surprise that his fellow officers left the control tower for the lifeboats soon after their leader abandoned his position. Not only did they lose trust in their leader's ability to lead, they lost confidence in themselves as well.

THE MIRROR PRINCIPLE

The day every parent dreads is the day their child uses a swear word in public. We have all seen it happen, or it has happened to you as a parent. You are with friends or family, and your small child blurts out something incredibly inappropriate. You are deeply embarrassed as you try and quiet your oblivious child. Your friends nervously laugh and resume their conversation. When your child sees the attention she is getting, she continues to use the word. You continue to shush her.

Here's the thing. Your child has no moral meaning attached to the word. To her, the word is just as useful as ball, dog, or milk. She is not thinking the action of using the word is offensive. She only knows what she sees.

The behavior of mirroring begins early in our lives and never ends.

We see it in body language mirroring. Next time you find yourself in the middle of a deep conversation, look down at your arms. Do they match the arm pattern of your conversation partner? For example, are both of your arms crossed? Are they sitting in your lap? Are they occupied in your pockets? The same is true with the actions of your organization. They will mirror the language, the activities, the work ethic, the priority, and the motivation that the leaders embody. The action of the leader not only demonstrates what is appropriate, but it also permits for the followers to act that way as well.

You must be what you want them to be.

Dr. Fast's study found something much more sinister about the human mind. The study went on to explain that "blaming others" is a mechanism by which individuals protect a positive self-image. No one wishes to believe themselves as lazy, lying, or unworthy of love. Therefore, we create a narrative in our minds that we are none of those things. Dr. Fast's study demonstrated that if the participants had a high sense of self-image, they were less likely to blame others for their failures.[32]

ESSENTIALS TO TAKING RESPONSIBILITY

If you're asking "When does it become their responsibility?", you aren't asking the right question. Consider asking yourself what you have done to produce the values, responsibility, and duty within them that you desire to see. Both employees and employers should consider it an honor to work together. But the key is to work together. The Mirror Principle determines how your organization will run: Your employees will mirror the behavior that you exhibit. If you take extreme ownership and exhibit responsibility in all aspects of your role, your employees will do the same. If you do not trust your people and blame others for problems, they will do the same. In the workplace, leaders must move first. If you walk towards them, they'll move towards you. It doesn't work the other way around.

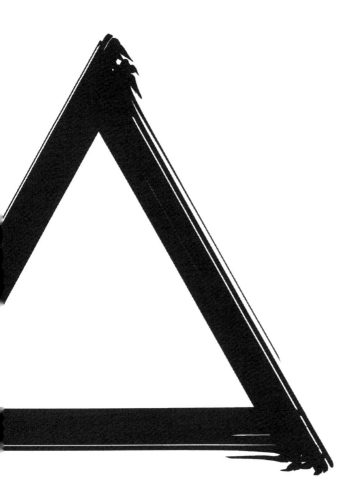

PART 2:
THE PARADIGM
The Simple Truths That Motivate Us All

9

SEE THEM FIRST

We want to show you how to get a free drink on an airplane.

Between speaking at conferences weekly and working with clients around the world, we spend a lot of time in the air and even more time at airports. Brian has come up with what he calls his "Scientific Method for Getting a Free Drink in Coach." For those who don't drink, always fly first class, or fly private, you can join us ordinary folk for a moment and still catch the principles.

Getting a free drink in coach starts before you get to your seat. If you're sitting in front of the plane, the flight attendant covering your seat is usually standing at the front of the airplane as you're boarding. Here is when step number one begins. As you're stepping onto the aircraft, make direct eye contact with the flight attendant, give a genuine smile and say, "How are you today?" in an upbeat tone. When he or she responds and asks you the same, give a genuine answer. The key is to be authentic and to be memorable.

Food and beverage service will begin as the plane is close to cruise altitude. Now for step number two. When the flight attendant gets to you and is handing you a drink napkin, smile and say, "Hey! What's your name?" After they state their name, genuinely say, "Thank you for helping me today."

Then, he or she will ask, "Anything to drink?" Order water and let them finish up the first pass of food and beverage service. After the first pass is complete and they've put away the beverage cart (and the handheld payment terminal), wait until the same flight attendant walks by. Make eye contact, take out your headphones, and nicely say, "Hey, [First Name], I think I might want some red wine. What do you have?"

Their response might be, "We have pinot noir and cabernet." Your answer should be, "Cabernet sounds good." Notice the casual, somewhat undecided language. This is intentional. Minutes later, they will return with your drink. When they do, say, "Thank you so much, [First Name]." Nine out of 10 times this works, and they don't ask for your credit card. If you've done it right, they'll pay attention to your glass and later ask if you'd like another. That will be free, too.

Here's the principle: Before asking anything of anyone, you must see them first. To see your employees means to show them that they matter.

In the "Scientific Method for Getting a Free Drink in Coach," here's how Brian "sees them first." First, he makes a genuine effort to ask the flight attendant how their day is going as he boards the aircraft. Second, Brian asks for their name and expresses gratitude for their help on the flight. Third, to eliminate the perception of ulterior motives, he does not ask for a free drink right after expressing gratitude. He never uses the word "free" at all. Brian then lets them reflect on the positive interaction as they finish up the first pass of the food and beverage service. Then, without being too direct, he asks what kind of red wine is available.

By taking a genuine interest in their day, he has recognized that they are a human being with feelings. By asking for their name, he has triggered the part of their brain that houses their very identity and personality. As Dale Carnegie said, "A person's name is to him or her the sweetest and most important sound in any language."[1]

By not asking for anything (other than water) after expressing gratitude for their help, he has said, "I recognize that you're serving me right now, but I'm not entitled to anything." Finally, by casually saying, "I think I might want some red wine," he's creating a situation in which he will probably get what he wants (a complimentary drink). However, he is still giving the flight attendant a choice in what they will do.

Before asking anything of anyone, you must see them first. Your employees aren't simply pursuing a paycheck. Your people are seeking significance. The pursuit of significance is the pursuit to matter. The journey to significance starts and ends with helping people.

To meaningfully impact others, your employees must know their specific purpose and how to use it. If you want to accomplish great things with your people, you must see them first. You must show them that they matter. For that, you need to know one thing: their purpose. Purpose is the cornerstone of the entire "Keep Them Longer" method. It is the secret to finding, building, and leading a great organization. It is the one thing that's guaranteed to create a positive and loyal work culture.

Your role is to help your people discover their individual purposes and show them how to live it out at work. Before you can do that, you must find it for yourself. We're going to show you how with our *PurposeFinder Formula™*.

HOW TO FIND YOUR PURPOSE

When we discuss the power of purpose at work, we get thoughtful nods from the leaders in the room. It's as if they are saying, "Yes, of course. We know." When we turn the tables and ask how they help their employees find and apply their purpose at work, we get blank stares. You see, purpose—at least how the Western World understands it—is an elusive catch-all for feeling good about yourself. Its definition ends up conflated with passion or becoming so broad that it is meaningless to the individual.

There is a specific process by which you and your people can discover their purpose. It's called *The PurposeFinder Formula™*, and it's the subject of our next book. The dictionary definition of purpose is, "The reason for which something or someone exists."[2] That definition is helpful if you're writing a college paper.

But for you and the purposes of understanding your people and keeping them longer, we want you to see purpose like this: "Purpose is what you have inside of you to help others." In turn,

"Fulfillment is the result of helping others with what you have inside of you."

Your people are searching for significance. Here's how that works:

- To find significance, they must know that they matter.
- To know they matter, they must know they're making a difference.
- To know they're making a difference, they must impact others.
- To impact others, they must know what they have to impact others.

What your employees have to influence others are their purpose and its specific components. If they use their purpose to impact others, they'll experience fulfillment, not just fleeting happiness. Your employees will experience the kind of fulfillment that is transformational. That's because fulfillment is the result of helping others with their purpose. So basically, your people need to know what they have to offer the world. We're not just talking about what's on their résumé.

After conducting extensive research on purpose in life and work, thousands of engagement surveys, and dozens of in-depth focus groups, we've discovered that there are four distinct parts to your purpose:

1. Natural Talents
2. Learned Skill Sets

3. Passion
4. Origin Story

The components inside the parentheses are your "Purpose Core"—the combination of your Natural Talents, Learned Skill Sets, and Passion. Your Origin Story is your "Marketplace Multiplier." We'll explain why after we define the pieces.

$$PURPOSE$$
$$=$$
$$(Natural\ Talents + Learned\ Skill\ Sets + Passion)$$
$$\times$$
$$Origin\ Story$$

Figure 3: The PurposeFinder Formula™

NATURAL TALENTS

Natural Talents are what you naturally do well. Natural Talents are innate, already on the inside, and don't require education or experience. You may recognize them in yourself. You can easily see them in your colleagues. For example, it may be obvious which of your associates have natural gifts for leadership, empathy, problem-solving, execution, and communication. If you have children, you may notice natural athleticism or the ability to build things from limited resources.

- **Ask this question to discover your #1 Natural Talent**: "What is the most obvious talent that I can recall having, even at a young age?"

LEARNED SKILL SETS

Unlike Natural Talents, Learned Skill Sets require education or life experience to acquire. Perhaps you went to school for business and developed expertise in supply chain management or mergers and acquisitions. Maybe you studied human resources and developed expertise in compensation and benefits. Learned Skill Sets aren't only acquired in school. They're developed through self-study, life experience, and professional certifications.

For example, maybe you learned how to code on YouTube or took an online course on reselling books and furniture online. Perhaps you got your real estate or certified financial planner license. These are all examples of Learned Skill Sets. These, along with your job history, are likely featured on your LinkedIn or résumé. Know this too: Learned Skill Sets often get acquired as a result of first recognizing Natural Talents. For example, if you were a natural communicator, perhaps you studied broadcasting or English literature.

- **Ask this question to discover your #1 Learned Skill Set**: "What is the top skill that I have pursued in life, work, or studies?"

PASSION

Passion is another elusive subject. Its dictionary definition is "a strong or extravagant fondness, enthusiasm, or desire for anything."[3] While helpful, that doesn't explain Passion as it relates to you. Passion is more than just the enjoyment of something. We often see folks confuse Passion with a hobby. You may enjoy spending weekends gardening or watching football, but that does not mean it is the passion that drives you.

Another issue is that most people confuse Passion with Purpose and make the mistake of only being led by Passion. The result is a Passion for something in which they don't have Natural Talent. So you might get someone passionate about music but passionately bad at singing. If you don't believe me, go and watch old American Idol tryouts and plug your ears.

Or, you may get someone who would call themselves "passionate" about coffee who wants to start a coffee shop but is horrible at business and leading themselves without a boss. Maybe they just like coffee but harbor Natural Talents and Learned Skill Sets in other things. Purpose includes Passion, but Passion alone is not enough.

Our definition of Passion is the problem, injustice, or opportunity in the world that fires you up and for which you're willing to sacrifice.

Passion develops through something you experience. In turn, that inspired and equipped you to help others through the same thing. For example, you may have discovered how to overcome depression. Now you're passionate about helping others do the same. Perhaps you got laid off and learned how to turn your career around. Now you like assisting others in landing their dream jobs. Maybe you struggled to lose weight, but after adopting a healthy diet, you have lost 50 pounds. Now you love helping others make smart food decisions and getting healthy.

As for the "sacrifice" part of the definition, your willingness (or unwillingness) to sacrifice for your passion and, ultimately, your purpose, is a great way to test whether you're on the right track.

- **Ask these questions to discover your #1 Passion**: "What is the problem in the world that you want to see solved? When you see people who don't know something, don't have something, or aren't able to do something, does it make you sad or angry? Does it inspire you to action?"

ORIGIN STORY

We often see individuals get discouraged halfway through *The PurposeFinder Formula*™ because their Natural Talents, Passion, and Learned Skill Sets feel so generic (that's because they aren't specific enough in their answers). They see others in their industry or even in their family who share the same traits, and they feel like there is nothing special for them to bring.

That's where Origin Story comes in. It is an essential part of your Purpose. It's your competitive advantage in life and the marketplace. That's because it's unique to you. No one else has it, and no one else can copy it.

The concept of Origin Story is most associated with how comic book heroes got their superpowers. It's the nerdy Peter Parker getting bit by a radioactive spider and then transforming into Spiderman with superhuman strength. It is Bruce Wayne losing his parents as a child and embracing the symbol of the bat because it is the one thing that scared him most. We are drawn to these Origin Stories because we love the story arch of a tragedy turning into a superpower.

Your Origin Story is the moment or series of moments that built you and gave you your "superpowers."

While they can be, these moments aren't usually positive experiences. They're experiences that put you under pressure—the kind of pressure that makes a diamond and produces brilliance. Perhaps you experienced sexual assault and it gave you a heart for the victimized. Maybe you went through a divorce and it taught you how to fully appreciate relationships and be grateful for the individuals in your life. Or, perhaps you nearly died in a car accident and it took six months to walk again. Now you have an incredible overcomer spirit. For Brian, going through a divorce and a job layoff in the same month taught him how to discover and use his purpose. That gave him the ability to help others find and use theirs.

- **Ask this question to discover your Origin Story**: "What event, or series of events, shaped the way that I see the world? What is the hardest or most impactful moment of my life?"

IT'S ABOUT MORE THAN "WHY"

Knowing why someone does something is extremely important. We know that "Why?" is a powerful question. Employees buy into the vision and goal when we lead by explaining why before what or how.

However, knowing the "why" isn't enough.

You may know why getting more sleep makes you more productive, but that doesn't mean you turn off the television and get in bed by 10 p.m. You may know why putting on a seatbelt saves lives, but that doesn't mean you remember to buckle up every time you get in a car. You may understand why it's crucial to eat vegetables and drink more water, but that doesn't mean you will pick broccoli over a burger at dinner tonight.

When we limit our questions of purpose to someone's "why," we never get to the application of their purpose in our organization. That is why the process of *The PurposeFinder Formula*™ ends with their Origin Story rather than begins with it. We must discover their unique skill sets and passions along with their stories to effectively utilize them at work. We will break down in the next chapter exactly how to do just that.

When you help them live out their purpose at work, you not only see them today, you are a part of who they are becoming tomorrow.

USING PURPOSE AT WORK

When you look at the components of purpose, you realize that you and your team have four things to offer at work. Most companies only leverage one. They leverage the Learned Skill Set part of *The PurposeFinder Formula*™.

When they do that, they limit the potential contribution of the employee to just the tasks that they can accomplish. But when organizations tap into the full spectrum of their employees, including the Origin Story that drives them, they experience incredible results.

It is a myth that you can't talk about hard things at work. Remember Phil's story from the beginning of the book? We helped him discover his #1 Natural Talent, empathy, his #1 Learned Skill Set, training, and his #1 Passion, helping people feel accepted and loved. And when we got to his Story, saving his roommate from committing suicide, he had finally come to the point of personal discovery. Phil never knew that everything that had happened in his life had positioned him for success. He was unafraid of sharing his most powerful life moment, and it transformed his relationships and his influence instantaneously.

We have sanitized the workplace to only include discussions about the weather or traffic in fear of exclusion, in some cases, or over-inclusion in others. Removing the humanity from our work cultures is causing our workplace relationships to rot and hurting our bottom lines.

As employers, we're getting it wrong.

We enable employees to gossip about the new boss but discourage employees from discussing their divorce at work. We allow team members to complain about a new process or program but punish employees for taking time off to handle issues at home. We expect employees to refer people to come work for us, but don't take the time to learn why they chose to work with us. We ask employees to give 100 percent but only ever use 25 percent of who they are.

Each of us is a complex human being. The lines between our public lives (what we let others know) and our personal lives (what actually goes on) are never clear. A fight you have with a spouse on the drive into work bleeds into your productivity for the rest of the day. A sick child keeps you distracted through your meetings. It's not just the tough stuff people worry about. Research shows the average bride-to-be spends 2.6 hours a week at work planning her wedding![4]

If you are worried that your reception desk will start looking like a psychologist's office, it won't. The culture will self-regulate what is and what is not appropriate at work. That is, as long as you create a culture of trust that embraces authenticity and celebrates the journey your employees are on. College application papers often start with a writing prompt asking what challenges the applicant has experienced and how it makes them qualified to attend the school. It is often the deciding factor for why someone is accepted despite poor grades or less-than-stellar test scores.

When we ask employers to engage with the stories of their employees, it is not a breach of trust that causes a potential compliance complaint. It is a bridge of trust that leads to higher levels of engagement and meaning.

To appropriately see your employees, use the following conversation starters:

- Why did you choose this industry?
- What has most influenced your career path thus far?
- If you feel comfortable with sharing, what would you say is the biggest challenge you have overcome in your life?
- Who has had the most significant impact on your life and why?
- What project have you worked on recently that you loved doing?
- What project have you worked on recently that you dreaded doing?
- What would make you come in early or stay late?

ESSENTIALS TO SEEING THEM FIRST

Before you keep them longer, you must see your employees. Seeing your employees means that you take the time to help them discover their purpose. Purpose is what is inside of you to help others. Leaders who connect the purpose of the company to the purpose of the individual never have a problem keeping them longer. The secret to helping employees discover their purpose is to utilize *The PurposeFinder Formula*™.

This process includes identifying their #1 Talent, #1 Learned Skill Set, #1 Passion, and their Origin Story. Their Origin Story is their "Marketplace Multiplier." It is what uniquely sets them apart and what will drive them to work harder and longer for you. Your employees want to find significance in their work. The more significance they find in work, the more meaning they will discover in what they do while working for you.

10

GROW THEM
ALWAYS

"We can't expect [them] to do [their] best at work if [they've] got problems at home." [1]

–S. Truett Cathy, late CEO & Founder of Chick-fil-A

When Brinker International promoted Dom Perry to Vice President of People Works, the casual dining powerhouse that owns Chili's and Maggiano's, he was already an employee-culture icon. But despite the fast-moving nature of the industry, Dom admits that he and his team needed to adapt. The training was paper-based. "It wasn't being leveraged. We were having a hard time executing on the program—plus, there was no way to measure the ROI," he said.

It wasn't enough to be an industry leader in the early 2000s. They would need to adapt the training and technology to prepare their team members for service better.

Today, if you become a new team member at Chili's, you will access your training via your smartphone. You will be trained on running the cash register via a video game. You will be trained on interacting with challenging customers by watching a video and

151

answering a series of questions that resemble a digital decision tree. Chili's' training infuses all five of Gallup's Wellbeing Essential Elements because, as Dom puts it, "Wellbeing is more than a program."

"You feel like it's a game, but you're learning," Dom says about their updated micro-learning approach. Even more exciting, their results translate to positive guest response, higher employee retention, and a more engaged workforce. Brinker restaurants' turnover among hourly employees is 30 percent lower than the industry average.

Rick Badgley, Chief Administrative Officer at Brinker, spearheaded this new-age approach to training. Rick is a winsome figure, with an impressive pedigree as an executive with brands including TOMS, Starbucks, and Wyndham Hotels. When Rick joined the Brinker ranks three years ago, he had a robust theology about employees. If Brinker was going to adapt, they had three choices: buy talent, borrow talent, or build talent.

Buying talent is expensive. You have to constantly out-compensate your competitors, which can lead to inflated salaries and financial losses. Borrowing talent is tricky. You have to aggressively recruit from your competitors, which can be stressful and exhausting. Or, you can build talent. Building talent means investing in your people, recruiting internally, and constructing rich development plans for all employees.

But it would take a clear strategy to move fast. Perhaps more than a strategy, it would require patience and humility. The two-year journey of research and development included analyzing their development programs and completely redesigning every aspect of their recruiting and training. They played with augmented reality and virtual reality to simulate experiential training.

Countless studies show, and common sense affirms, that adults learn better by doing versus sitting in a classroom. The Brinker development team decided to emphasize what they knew worked. Now their training has a 70-20-10 split. Seventy percent of the training is experiential, both in-person and simulated via technology. Twenty percent is exposure to information and job shadowing. Only ten percent is in traditional classroom education.

Nine months into implementation, the team started to see wins. They had gone from 35 percent internal promotion to 75 percent internal promotion. "You have to always be evolving," Dom said of his most important lesson on the journey. "You have to listen to your team every step of the way ... If you connect to them, there's no more loyal person," he said.

Chili's and Maggiano's are looking for potential instead of experience in new hires. Despite being in an industry ridden with turnover, Chili's has proven that growing your employees will keep them longer. It will also get you national recognition and make you a fan-favorite with your customers. The Chili's transformation is what happens when you combine science and systems with humanity and heart. It is not in the absence of training that culture thrives. It is not in the existence of training that culture thrives. The right training for your team will make all the difference. A healthy culture can only thrive in an environment where good things grow and dangerous things die.

If you grow the person, you grow the employee. If you grow the people, you grow the organization.

WHAT IT MEANS TO GROW THEM

Chick-fil-A is notorious for advocating for the wellbeing of their people. Whether it is giving their employees Sundays off, offering relationship counseling, or teaching basic manners, the chicken sandwich superpower has made billions from growing their people first.

The men and women that work for you were people before they were employees. If you help them live a better life at home, they will live a better life at work. Now, you may be thinking, "But isn't this just common sense?" Perhaps it is. Let us ask you this. What is common sense?

Is common sense how to change the oil in your truck? Is it how to balance a checkbook? Is it how to ask someone out on a date? What was "common sense" for one generation may be irrelevant for another. Brian decided to change the oil of our SUV. When he went to check the dipstick, what he found was simply an oil cap. A quick Google search on his smartphone revealed that our vehicle has an electronic dipstick. The car must be hooked up to a computer and the oil level measured digitally.

When was the last time you wrote a check? Unless you do payroll for a company (even that is usually done through electronic transfer), you may not remember. Balancing your checkbook was once a week occurrence done on kitchen tables across the country. Now you can retrieve all of your financial information from a convenient smartphone app.

Even dating has become polluted by technology. If you want to ask a girl or a guy out on a date, instead of walking up to them and asking for their number, you find them online and send a message. And that may only happen after sufficiently looking through their photos to make sure that they aren't some strange psycho. Common sense has changed. We have different skills now than we did twenty or thirty years ago.

We cannot expect incoming employees to come equipped with the same type of "common sense" that older generations possessed. Chick-fil-A knows this well. They hire mostly young people. Those young people do not come into their restaurants already saying, "My pleasure" and, "It's a beautiful day at Chick-fil-A." The Chick-fil-A team knows they must develop those skills inside of their people. What kind of skills should be developed? Any skills your employee needs to thrive.

You may say that you are committed to your employees' development. But what are you doing to support that mission? Do your employees see you growing them more than they hear you talk about growing them? There is growing research that shows employers who invest in relationship and stress management training have healthier, happier employees.[2] That makes sense. If your employees are having a hard time outside of work, they will have a hard time at work. But what's the return on investment?

Wellbeing at work has rightfully gained prominent billing in the people management space. Workplace wellbeing programs respect the multi-dimensional lives of employees. It includes physical health, mental health, spiritual health, and relational health.

"Presenteeism" is when employees come to work despite being sick, distracted, or in some way not able to adequately perform their role. It costs businesses ten times more than absenteeism. According to the World Health Organization's Workplace Health and Productivity Study, employees confess to being unproductive due to personal distraction 57.5 days per year.[3]

Distracted employees are more prone to make mistakes and have accidents at work. They hurt production, customer service, and internal morale.

One notable research project estimates that marriage and relationship issues cost American businesses $6 billion in decreased productivity. The relationship between productivity and personal issues is so carefully studied that a formula has been created to measure the correct cost. For an employee making $20 an hour, the cost of their divorce on the company is over $8,000. And not only that, employees who experience divorce lose on average of 168 hours of work time. That's like taking four extra weeks of vacation in one calendar year.[4]

It isn't just relationships. Mental health is costing companies big, too. Depressed employees cost companies $44 billion annually.[5] Healthcare costs skyrocket as emotionally unhealthy individuals are more likely to get sick, miss work, and abuse medication.

We met Jason Brown speaking at a large leadership conference in Dallas. Jason is a put-together guy. From his bright blue blazer coordinating with his eyes to his perfectly groomed hair and smile, Jason stands out. We got to talking while simultaneously having small microphones pinned to our lapels and wired down our backs. Jason is the Chief Marketing Officer of Marketplace Chaplains, an organization that places chaplains inside of companies.

Companies offering chaplains to their employees? Having never heard of such a concept, we needed to hear more. Marketplace Chaplains was founded in 1984 to support the emotional health of employees, long before "wellbeing" was a trend. They have grown every year since their inception and serve every state in the country. Chaplains in the program make weekly visits to worksites and serve many major brands' clients. Chaplains sit with parents struggling to cope with the loss of a child. They make house calls for depressed and emotionally distressed employees. They provide training and resources on parenting teenagers, financial wellness, caring for aging parents, and much more. Chaplains even help calm workplace frustrations by being a neutral third party who can listen to both sides of the story without an agenda.

The results? A custom home builder cut their turnover in half, from 40 percent to 20 percent. A national logistics company increased engagement from 52 percent to 72 percent in less than two years. A large hotel chain and quick change oil corporation have seen dramatic decreases in sick leave. Plus, the chaplains report stopping several suicides every month. When you ask Jason why this is happening, his answer is simple. "This is preventative maintenance, not crisis response," he said.

Treating employees like whole people, offering wellbeing resources that go beyond health and fitness, is an essential aspect of keeping them longer.

SEE THEM BEFORE YOU GROW THEM

You can't grow your people if you haven't seen them first.

We were brought in to help a major automotive brand retain their Millennial employees. Despite the internationally renowned reputation of the company, their internal culture needed some help. We conducted focus groups with their young and new employees and then put together a report for the leadership. The results of the report showed what we already knew. The company was divided between leadership and employees. The two were not on the same page.

There were two shining examples of this. We asked the Millennials what they would like more training on. The leadership had already assumed they would say something like systems processes, or that they needed more support on the technical side. Nope. The next generation of employees requested training on time management, managing up, and conflict resolution—soft skills. Professional development. The top and possibly the most surprising request? They wanted training on how the business worked. Any preconceived notion that these "kids" just wanted a paycheck and more happy hours were out the window.

Then there was the second big revelation. We asked what current training they most enjoyed. There were blank stares. Before we conducted the focus group, the leaders briefed us on their current training and development opportunities. Like most large organizations, the company offered many course options and posted training and development opportunities on their intranet. The participation level was frustratingly low, and the assumption was that Millennials don't like to learn. Wrong again. The Millennials we interviewed were not aware of the scores of courses currently being offered by the company. Despite the time, effort, and budget the leaders were investing in training, it was going unnoticed.

Here's the principle. If the training is not relevant and not apparent, it will go unused. The only way that you can discover what is appropriate and apparent is to ask your people what they need and how they want it delivered.

You cannot grow what you do not see. So if you skipped the last chapter, or you need a refresh, go back and visit the principles. Understanding your people first develops the trust and buy-in required to grow your employees properly. When you see them, you show them that they matter, that they have a purpose, and that they can live out their mission at your company. That's the necessary foundation for growing them.

WHY YOU DON'T NEED MORE ENGAGEMENT

Can we ask you a question? How do you define engagement?

Would you include something about productivity, fulfillment, passion, community? Would you tell a story or use a personal anecdote? We have found that individuals who define engagement in their terms are most likely to be engaged themselves.

Can we ask you another question? How do the people on your team define engagement? Is it the same way that you define it? Like we mentioned in our chapter on the myth of "needing more engagement," most organizations do a great job of complaining about engagement and a terrible job of doing something about it.

The disconnect in definitions is hurting the very thing you are trying to measure. Most human resources departments track engagement like The Weather Channel tracks a tornado. Surveys dispatch at a constant flow and data begins to pile up. At any given moment, everything could be upset by a hurricane of voluntary turnover or bad reviews on Glassdoor.

The modern workforce is experiencing an engagement epidemic. Gallup has been leading the field when it comes to measuring engagement at work. Their annual State of the Global Workforce study has become the go-to of the workforce world. In 2017, Gallup found across 155 countries that only 15 percent of employees worldwide are engaged at work. That means 85 percent of employees globally are disengaged or actively disengaged at work.[6]

In America, the numbers are better, but nothing to brag about. Only 33 percent of American employees are engaged at work, leaving 66 percent disengaged or actively disengaged.[7] If you're in America, this means that there is a 66 percent chance that your team members are not doing their best work. For productivity, this means companies have a lot of room for improvement and a lot of opportunities to increase revenues.

So how do the experts define engagement?

Chairman and CEO of Gallup, Jim Clifton, says it's development. Just asking, "Is there someone at work who encourages your development?" separates enthusiastic, high-performing workers from low-performing, miserable ones.[8] In other words, if you want a more engaged workforce, your success comes down to whether or not your employees feel that someone is committed to their improvement.

Seeing your people is essential. Growing your people is vital. What's fascinating, however, is that most companies don't have employee engagement and development programs beyond benefits and pay. We hear that all the time. Companies continue to focus on the paycheck, but what employees want is purpose. That isn't to say that fair pay doesn't matter. It does. Fair pay, proper benefits, and physically and emotionally safe work environments are the baseline. They are the hygiene standard. It's the right thing to do to respect your employees. Your company will never be voted a top place to work because you do what is right. You will be recognized as an employer of choice because you do what is extraordinary.

START IN THE MIDDLE

So how do you go about growing your people? First, you need to work on you. You cannot give what you do not possess. Before implementing this process on others, you must do it on yourself. You need to know that you're valuable, that you have a purpose, and how to live out your purpose at work. Better yet, you need to experience the transformation of yourself and let your employees witness the change.

After you grow yourself, you need capable leaders in the middle of the organization. Most companies think that growing your people means developing new and frontline employees. They skip right over the growth of their middle managers and train from the bottom up.

Mid-level managers are the most neglected and undertrained class of employees today. They get wedged between Baby Boomers delaying retirement and Millennials eager to take their jobs. It is no wonder that this class of employees proves to be the most unhappy at work.[9]

Consider how you are offering growth opportunities for the middle of your corporate structure.

Before you can grow your newest employees, you need managers in the middle that view employees as assets. These managers must be trained to become leaders that give more than they take. Leaders that recognize the importance of growing their employees will expand their own opportunities as well.

WHAT TO TRAIN THEM ON

It was halfway through our interview when we finally asked, "What is an example of you doing it well?"

We were speaking with the human resources director for a large manufacturing company about their onboarding program. She was becoming frustrated with the questions about how they recruit and train new employees. The head of human resources was aware that they needed to improve, but just the thought of creating another program brought on heavy sighs. We finally asked a question we have found profoundly reveals the truth.

We asked, "What part of your job are you most proud of?"

She paused a moment or two and then responded. "Our intern program is pretty great," she said. We asked her to share how they recruit and train their interns. They developed relationships with local schools. They provided informational material about the industry, assuming the Millennials were unaware of the opportunity in front of them. It was unlike anything they had done before. They created a training cohort for the interns to join. They hosted luncheons with the president of the company. They had scheduled activities outside of the office and interactive learning programs. The human resource director was proud of this program—and she should be. But why is it that when we asked how they train their employees, she couldn't share a single example?

Brian calls this the "Kitten Phenomenon."

Let's say you are in the middle of deep work. You have been working in a flow on a project, and it is going well. Finally. Then, out of the blue, someone places a fluffy orange-striped kitten on your desk. Even if you are not a cat person, you would stop what you are doing and admire the kitten. It's too cute not to! You would pick it up carefully and pet its ridiculously fluffy coat. When it unknowingly ruins your sweater by climbing up your chest, you would be annoyed but understanding. It's a baby. It doesn't know any better. Then, you would find a safe place for the kitten while you do your work. That, or blow off the rest of the day and play with your new fluffy friend.

Now, let's say you are in the middle of deep work and a fully grown cat jumps on your desk. What would you do? Would you pick up the cat and play with it gently? Would you swat it away with frustration? The way you treat a kitten is very different than how you treat a fully grown cat.

Brian calls it the "Kitten Phenomenon" because companies treat interns like kittens but their employees like cats. The same activity may be slightly annoying and forgivable for some but unacceptable and inappropriate for others.

Companies put on a good face for their interns, and they should. They should seek to recruit the next generation actively. They should think creatively about how they train young people. They should provide extracurricular activities for interns to participate in together. They should have structure, mentors, and training systems. What if we trained all employees like we train interns? What if we thought this creatively about how we can actively engage and entertain them? What if we treated their experience as necessary to the success of our future because it is?

Organizations must train the whole person in order to keep them longer. Whole-person training programs are designed to serve the multi-dimensional aspects of your employees' lives. We discuss at length what to include in whole-person training programs in Chapter Fourteen.

Growing your employees is essential to keeping them longer. Companies that invest in comprehensive training experience returns on investment that go beyond retention. As a leader, you must grow yourself first and invest in your people always. When you do, your people will stay because of who you are making them to be, not because of what you are paying them to do.

ESSENTIALS TO GROW THEM

Great leaders grow the whole person. They realize that employees were people before they ever received a paycheck. As people, their personal lives influence their professional lives, and vice versa. The most effective training includes equipping employees to thrive in work and life. Great organizations offer training that includes compliance, personal success, professional success, and leadership. Great training programs offer clear outcomes for participants and invite employees at all levels to actively manage their professional development.

11

INVOLVE
THEM
TODAY

"Responsibility equals accountability equals ownership. And a sense of ownership is the most powerful weapon a team or organization can have." [1]

**–Pat Summitt, Legendary Tennessee
Women's Basketball Coach**

The first digital camera existed before the personal computer, but you probably didn't know that. The camera weighed eight pounds and took twenty-three seconds from the moment the picture was taken to the moment you could view it on a screen. The resulting image was black and white and 100 pixels by 100 pixels. [2]

For 1975, that was pretty impressive. But why did it take until 1990 for the first digital camera to hit the market? [3] Because Kodak didn't want you to know about the breakthrough or the man who made it happen. In doing so, Kodak violated the third principle of the Keep Them Longer method: Involve Them.

In 1973, Steven Sasson graduated from Rensselaer Polytechnic Institute and went to work for Kodak. Steve is the kind of guy that you would expect to invent something. He is smart, measured in his tone, and when we talked to him, incredibly humble. As he talks, he flows between tech-talk and nostalgic personal reflection. At the time, Steve's assignment was to find out if there was any use for the charged coupled device, or "CCD." The CCD was invented only a couple years earlier. The CCD is a sensor that converts light into an electrical signal. For Steve, this relatively unimportant assignment led to one of the most significant breakthroughs in photography.

It also became an early precursor to the cameras in our phones and today's social media apps such as Facebook and Instagram. After all, without digital photography, social media would be pretty dull. In a 2015 interview with *The New York Times*, Steve said:

> "Hardly anybody knew I was working on this because it wasn't that big of a project. It wasn't a secret. It was just a project to keep me from getting into trouble doing something else, I guess."[4]

As Steve got to work, he decided to try and capture an image with the CCD. And while the device could convert light into an electrical signal, it couldn't store the result. To remedy this, he incorporated two other computing processes: digitalization and random access memory (otherwise known as "RAM"). Digitalization is the process of converting electronic pulses into numbers. Numbers, specifically 1s and 0s, are the basis for all computing and is known as "Binary Code." RAM is simply a type of computer memory.

Together with a few other components, Steve had built the first digital camera. Nobody at Kodak seemed to care. He presented the prototype to groups of executives from around the company by taking their group picture and immediately showing them the result on a screen. What happened? No parties and no Apple-esque launch keynotes. Just pushback.

Steve told *The New York Times*:

"They were convinced that no one would ever want to look at their pictures on a television set. Print had been with us for over 100 years; no one was complaining about prints, they were very inexpensive, and so why would anyone want to look at their picture on a television set?"[5]

That's undoubtedly ironic in the context of today.

Kodak had virtually monopolized the print photo industry—from the film, the chemicals for processing, to the paper. Why create something that eliminated the need for film and the chemicals—their cash cow? Since the executives determined that digital couldn't compete with print, they allowed Steve to continue his work but didn't take anything to market. Steve was also barred from talking about his invention or showing it to anyone outside of Kodak.

The one thing the executives did do, however, was secure the patent. So, the first digital camera was born in 1975 and received its first patent in 1978. Later, in 1989, Steve and a colleague created the first digital camera that works like today's professional digital cameras. Again, Kodak wasn't interested.

One year later, in 1990, the first digital camera hit the market, and the race to digital was on. Kodak (not Steve) made billions off the patent as companies paid them for the right to use it. But when the patent expired in 2007, Kodak had gotten into the digital game too late. Nobody had to pay them to use it anymore. By 2012, the company had filed for bankruptcy. Kodak's film and processing chemicals were no longer kings. The world had entered the digital photography era, and Kodak missed it.

As for Steve, Kodak used him, but they didn't involve him.

Kodak assigned him to understand the CCD. When he made one of the most significant discoveries in the history of photography, they shoved the breakthrough in a proverbial time capsule. The company made billions off the patent that Steve was responsible for and didn't work with him to invest in the future of the company after the patent expired. Involving him would have meant leveraging his skill sets (and, ideally, his purpose) at the highest level, not only to produce cash flow from the patent but to work with him to create Kodak's next cash cow. That way, Kodak could have survived the death of film.

Involving your talent is the third key to keeping your talent.

By seeing them, you're helping your employees find their purpose and why they matter. By growing them, you're telling your team that you care about their success and upward mobility. And by involving them, you're empowering them to be a part of a supportive community and demonstrating how their contribution is consequential.

TO INVOLVE MEANS WHAT YOU DO TOGETHER

See. Grow. Involve.

The sequence of seeing, then growing, then involving is by design. It was crafted after observing and overseeing countless corporate transformation stories. Before you give someone responsibility within an organization, they must be trained. Before you train someone, you must know what they bring to the table and where they need additional support.

So what does it mean to involve someone? Let's think about your hiring process. You did your best to recruit candidates, interview them, and select the best fit for your company or organization. You invested in top recruiters, spent hours poring over résumés and applications, and experienced your share of painful, time-sucking interviews. You trained them to do their job well and execute on their daily tasks.

But soon your investment took on a "set it and forget it" mindset.

Under the constraint of deadlines, internal politics, and leadership pressure, culture became fear-based. Transparency sunk to an all-time low, and managers fell prey to micro-managing talent, refusing to trust them except with small, low-risk tasks. Eventually, you recognized what most leaders do; "No wonder they're leaving in droves."

The third key to keeping them longer after seeing them and growing them is to involve them. To involve your employees is to focus on what you can accomplish together, not what you assign them to do. To involve them means to leverage their Natural Talents, Learned Skill Sets, Passion, and Origin Story in the accomplishment of your organizational goals. It also means empowering employees to accomplish their goals within the company.

Don't worry. It will pay off. Gallup suggests that by leveraging their strengths or natural talents alone, the chances of your talent disengaging at work is less than one percent.[6] Think about what that means for keeping them longer.

HOW TO INVOLVE THEM

There are a few elements to involving them. First, involving them requires giving your employees meaningful work on projects that matter. Yes, everyone must do things they don't want to do. However, your employees also need to work on projects and tasks that are aspirational. These are projects that grow and stretch them. Their job is connected to their identity. Plus, the quality of their experience in the position impacts their mental, physical, and emotional health.

Closely related to giving meaningful work is empowering them with task ownership. One of our good friends, Randy Wolken, is the President of the Manufacturers Association of Central New York (MACNY). He's a graduate of West Point and trained to lead in any situation. Randy has the kind of mind that you can see working, processing information, and storing it for later use. You're unsure what the information will be used for, but his jovial laugh and Boy Scout values assure you that it's in good hands.

It's no surprise to us that Randy's employee turnover is incredibly low. That's by design. He carefully and intentionally crafted MACNY to exude a realistic yet idyllic work culture. Part of the secret to his success is to involve new hires on day one by giving them task ownership on a meaningful project.

In doing so, Randy accomplishes a few things. One, he's immediately said, "I hired you for a reason. You're talented, and I want you to grow in those talents." Two, he's said, "I trust you, and I want us to work together on day one." Three, Randy has created an opportunity for this new hire to develop relationships within the culture of MACNY. Four, he's given them the chance to make mistakes, learn, and ask him questions.

He didn't assign them work and abandon them. Finally, instead of being the all-knowing leader handing down a project, he's put himself in the position of an encouraging coach—focused on growing his people to their highest potential. All of this generates a leader's greatest asset: trust. This is also good as we see new hires mentally making their long-term commitment decisions within the first few weeks of being hired. Tying them to the company with task ownership and meaningful involvement is a great first impression.

Involvement requires you to generate trust by distributing meaningful work on projects that matter, creating task ownership, and creating a community whereby employees can thrive and hold each other accountable.

Let's talk about how to do this practically. If you've already had an opportunity to see your employees first by helping them to discover their purpose, you know what you have to work with. You know their Natural Talents, their Learned Skill Sets, their Passions, and their Origin Stories. When assigning meaningful work and giving them task ownership, stay within the elements of their purpose and their core competencies.

HERE ARE THE FOUR STEPS TO INVOLVING THEM

1. Make Owned Tasks A Stretch, But Not A Leap.

If it's too much too soon, you may discourage your employees from getting involved. However, if the task is too simple, your employees will feel belittled and underutilized. Stretch tasks empower employees to seek assistance and wisdom from others, helping them to build community and peer-mentorship. It also serves as a confidence boost as they set a goal and work hard to achieve it, showing them that they have what it takes to grow within the company.

The tasks should stretch but not break your employees. Ensure that both you and your employees have clear expectations around what ideal involvement includes. You must clarify what level of involvement is achievable.

One of the greatest disappointments for a leader is handing off a task to an employee and having that person fail to make it happen. Perhaps the employee intentionally misrepresented their abilities. Or maybe they can do the work, but they don't effectively manage their time, so it never gets done. No matter the reason, trust is breached when expectations go unmet.

2. Connect Their Purpose and Core Competencies to the Project's Outcome.

Show employees how they're growing by working on a task. Many employees disregard a responsibility or even resent it because they don't see the big picture. If you have an employee who is passionate about solving problems, then show him or her how the project will further develop their problem-solving capabilities. Then show them how they can apply that skill set in different aspects of their job. If something has wired them to help people, show them how their work will help people and what kind of transformation it will produce. It's critical to make these connections to keep them longer.

3. Tie Tasks to Big Goals.

If it's all about the project and getting the project done for you, the leader, then you're taking, not giving. If you make it all about how the project will grow them in their purpose and their ability to prosper and help people, you're giving, not taking.

Big goals must get consensus at the beginning. Your employee will hold themselves accountable to the target because they're pulled toward something rather than pushed toward something.

Don't be afraid to work with your employees. Involve them in setting big goals. When you do, you give them a say in what they are working towards.

4. Make Their Roles and Responsibilities Clear.

There are two types of employees; those that ask for permission and those that expect forgiveness. Early in our company, we had one of each. One of our newly hired sales members was extremely eager to get to work. He had a great attitude, was taking to our materials quickly, and repeatedly shared his passion for the work we were doing. However, it became clear within weeks of hiring him that we needed to have a conversation about his role.

When we hire a new employee, we work with them on a document that outlines their roles and responsibilities. A role is like a hat you wear. It is the job you are doing at any given moment. A responsibility is a task or outcome that you oversee.

While out to lunch as a team, we ran into a friend of our new hire. He authentically gushed about his new job and introduced us as his business partners for a new company he was helping to start. Keep in mind, this young man was a sales rep, and no conversation occurred around equity or partner status. The company was five years old at the time and far from a startup. We didn't want to squash his newfound excitement, so decided only to address his blunder if it came up again.

It did.

After another mention of his new company and his inflated role in our existence, we set up a time to talk. Rather than giving him much needed clarity without first seeking to understand his perspective, we asked our hire how he saw his role. He said that it included sales, outreach, follow-up, and all the typical sales activities we had agreed on. We then asked what roles and responsibilities he believed a founding member would have. The light went off, and he understood where we were coming from. He apologized and stated he was just excited and didn't quite understand the appropriate way to talk about his new opportunity. We gave him some examples of how he can explain his role and encouraged him to keep sharing his experience with his community.

Our newest hire was involved. He was committed to our mission and feeling fulfilled every day. But more clarity was needed on what appropriate involvement meant. Involvement is not a permission slip to put the interns in charge of the annual budget. Involvement must be appropriate, prepared for, and accountable.

INVOLVEMENT REQUIRES COMMUNITY

We want to come back to the community element of involving your employees. Research on employee engagement shows that two factors contribute to the engagement level and the retainability factor of each employee. The first, as we've already discussed, is: Does the employee feel as if there is someone at work who encourages their development? The second is: Does the employee have a best friend at work?[7] By involving your employees with meaningful work and task ownership, you encourage their development. You've allowed them to develop deep and meaningful relationships within your culture.

Community is the essence of involvement. It is the dominant indicator of a healthy organization. There are six pillars of community that a good company must possess.

1. Trust

The survival of any community rises and falls on trust. When trust erodes, so does the success and survival of the group. Trust can be quickly built and even restored when you take the right approach.

Researchers at The Hunger Project were curious about whether there was a correlation between systemic poverty and trust within a community. They asked the question, "Do people who trust their neighbors and the government have a higher likelihood of lifting themselves out of poverty?" The study of U.S. and Bangladeshi neighborhoods measured two types of trust: generalized and community. Generalized trust is built through intense exposure to others and is built over time. Community trust occurs through quick and reliable transactions with others in the immediate environment.[8]

What they found was incredible. For two years, the project commissioned trust couriers—individuals who worked as intermediaries between the government and the community served. As the report on the results said:

"This involved representatives from the community working with the local government to make community-level decisions; for example, in the distribution of social benefits, the allocation of funds and resources for development projects, and the selection of people to use in publicly funded projects."[9]

At the end of the two years, individuals who built high levels of community trust were more likely to make wiser financial decisions that benefited their families long term. The study pointed out how unique this was, as most low-income individuals make short-term decisions and avoid investing in things like education, health, and finances. If systemic poverty can be reversed through trust-building activity, trust can seismically reduce turnover within an organization.[10]

2. Accountability

Involving someone without accountability is dangerous. Accountability is more than taking the blame when things go wrong. Nearly every election cycle, politicians are stumping on "keeping Washington accountable." Giant corporate behemoths are railed against for not being accountable to the environment but only caring about their profits. Accountability is not about deterring bad behavior. It is about enabling transformation and involving every member of the team in the result.

Accountability has become a dirty word. In reality, accountability is empowering. It means creating a goal and lining out what happens when things go wrong and when things go right.

The principle of involving them is built on the positive power of accountability. Accountability includes setting expectations, having agreed-upon results, and getting extreme clarity about the consequences.

3. Contribution

A community cannot exist where everyone takes. Remember The Water Cycle Principle. A community is built and sustained when everyone gives. Giving is the subject of our next chapter. But it is essential to involvement as well.

When you expect every person on the team to give, great things happen. Have you ever been in a meeting where the same person talks the entire time? It's exhausting. No one in the room feels that they have a voice. It doesn't feel ethical to have your voice talked over or, even worse, never acknowledged. Healthy communities create clear lines of expectations around giving. It is an ancient principle to give—everyone according to their ability, to everyone according to their needs. Communities that celebrate giving-inspired involvement are powerfully efficient.

4. Participation

You cannot supervise involvement. You have to experience it.

Healthy communities thrive because of robust and diverse involvement. Growing up in Northern California, Gabrielle spent summers and weekends driving into San Francisco. As soon as you descend into the bay, you immediately experience the colors, sounds, and even the smells of a bustling West Coast metropolis.

First-time visitors to California are often surprised at the vibe you get in the bay area. It is more United Nations than "Surfing USA."

Every neighborhood in San Francisco has its flair and flavor. You notice the buzzing tourism, sloshing sourdough chowder bowls, and knick-knack-lined shops along the pier. You also see the brightly colored lanterns and bilingual signs of the Chinese markets. You smell the smell of crushed garlic and texture of the mosaics along North Beach and the sparkling neighborhood known as Little Italy.

What made San Francisco so unique to Gabrielle as a child was how each neighborhood created its own community. It's as if each subculture was permitted to embrace who they were. The result is beautiful, and it is entirely dependent upon the principle of participation.

Participation requires action, but it also requires buy-in. When you participate, you immediately become tied to the result. If the success of your family business relies on keeping the street clean, you will go out of your way to sweep it each morning. In the same way, employees on teams must receive permission to participate and have their effort tied to a shared goal.

5. Transparency

Community requires transparency. Transparency means respecting someone enough to tell them the truth. Transparency is particularly important when difficult conversations need to happen.

The most turbulent times in an organization include when executives leave, company-wide layoffs, moving locations, and when there is an acquisition or merger. In each of these instances, employees are more at risk than ever of leaving. To keep them longer, leaders must overly communicate what is happening. No news is interpreted as bad news; so even if there are no updates to give, communicate regularly to the team. Communities that expect and celebrate transparency prepare for the good, bad, and everything in between. They can respond to difficulty and joy with the same amount of enthusiasm because there is trust and reliance.

Involving employees can only be done in a transparent environment. Directing an employee to do a task without expressing its importance or goal is not transparent. Moving an individual from one team to another without sharing how it will benefit them is not open. Switching up the agreed upon annual goals without first expressing that the team isn't hitting the numbers is not transparent.

6. Failure

Perhaps the most powerful pillar of community involvement is how a community treats failure. Failure is a principle, not a negative result. We discuss the impact of embracing failure at length throughout the book. It is important to highlight just how essential failure is to involving your employees.

More than creating accountability, failure permits your employees to get involved even when they don't have all of the answers. Failure embraces experimentation and creativity. It rewards attempts and reiterations. Failure is a given in any community. Failure, in reality, is feedback. Perfection isn't the expectation, which is why forgiveness flows more freely in our homes than in our offices.

If you are experiencing turnover amongst your creative and independent workers, it is because you have not given them the freedom to fail. That freedom is what will fuel the other pillars of community necessary to keep them longer.

ESSENTIALS TO INVOLVING THEM

Involving your employees comes down to what you will do together. In essence, it is the shift that happens when employees stop working for you and begin working with you. Involvement transforms employees from participants in the business to partners in its success. This step can only happen after you see and grow them. It gives employees the opportunity to apply their purpose and their training from the first two steps of the Keep Them Longer method. It entrusts every member of your team with the ability to pursue your mutual goals. Involvement means ownership of the success and the failure. To maximize your employees' involvement, create a community of mutual trust and respect where everyone's contribution is recognized and appreciated.

12

TEACH THEM
TO GIVE

It was Monday, July 18, 2016. When most of her peers were heading off to class or starting their job for the day, 23-year-old Abigail Flores was being airlifted after her liver ultimately failed.

Despite her young age, doctors said that she needed a transplant to survive. Abigail, a newlywed, had been on the waiting list for a transplant as she planned her wedding, got married, and started her new life. But now the doctors at Baylor Hospital in Dallas, Texas feared Abigail wouldn't survive the next 24 hours without a miracle.[1]

On that same day, 69-year-old Brenda Jones was rushed to the same hospital. It was good news for Brenda. Like Abigail, Brenda was also on the waiting list for a liver transplant. She had been waiting for a new liver every day for over a year. That day, Brenda's name was finally on top of the donor list. Two women with 46 years of life between them had nothing in common, apart from both facing the same fate if they did not receive a new liver.

There were multiple transplant procedures scheduled. When the doctors at Baylor Hospital witnessed how quickly Abigail was declining, they began checking to see if current donor recipients matched for the same liver. Brenda received a call at 3:30 a.m. The organ that she was being prepped to accept was the same type of liver Abigail needed—same blood type, same everything.[2]

The doctor explained the situation to Brenda, a great-grandmother. Go ahead with the scheduled operation or give up her place on the list for Abigail. Nothing prevented Brenda from taking the liver. And if she chose to give up her spot for Abigail, there was no promise of another match any time soon. Brenda's choice was simple: Give to another or keep what she deserved.

Brenda chose to go back on the waiting list, and Abigail lived. Brenda received another transplant opportunity just days later. What could have ended in a tragedy resulted in a miracle because Brenda gave first. From a story about life, death, and kindness comes a counterintuitive principle to keeping your top talent. When you give more than you take today, you maximize tomorrow's outcomes for everyone. When you take more than you give today—just the opposite occurs.[3]

GIVING DRIVES EVERYTHING

Brenda and Abigail remind us that humans are designed to give.

The free market is all about giving. Zig Ziglar said, "You will get all you want in life if you help enough other people get what they want."[4] If a company wants to expand its market share, it must give value through products to get and keep new customers. If a music artist wants to get a record deal, she must provide value to her audience through her music. If a restaurant wants to become profitable (most are not), it must give value to every customer that orders a dish.

You may be wondering if we advocate for giving and never charging for your products or services. Most individuals associate giving with charity, but that is only a small slice of what giving truly means. Having a "give value first" mindset does not mean that you give away everything for free. It means that you must invest in others before getting a return on that investment.

Here's a simple example. Brian loves his espresso machine. His Breville Infuser is a classic, manual espresso machine with a pressure gauge, built-in tamper, and steamer wand. It's gloss black with a chrome backsplash. The grinder is a Breville Smart Grinder Pro. It's gloss black, too, and has 60 different grind settings—including 30 settings just for espresso. The espresso machine was $500. The grinder was $200. Total: $700. He gladly paid for it. Brian gets incredible value out of his espresso machine. He gets monetary value, saving thousands of dollars in just four years on expensive coffee shop drinks. He also gets intangible value, enjoying the experience of "pulling shots" each morning.

Breville had to give value first. The Australian company had to create exceptional machines for people like Brian long before he was ever willing to hand over $700. They had to invest in the research and development of those machines. They had to fund the marketing capital to get Brian's attention and for him to see it in Williams-Sonoma. They had to make themselves completely vulnerable by producing and marketing machines that could have failed. Breville gave first. Because they gave first, Brian gave value back to Breville and is now giving them a shameless plug in this book.

The free market is about giving first and giving like crazy. So is leadership. As a leader, you must always give first. Do it right, do it authentically, and your employees will never hesitate to give value in return. To successfully keep your talent longer, you must do the following:

- Give first to your employees and future employees by finding them.
- Craft a position that appeals to their purpose and goals.
- Train them up to be the best that they can be.
- Coach them along as you give them meaningful work to do.

You must do nearly all of that before expecting anything in return. If you don't provide value to your employees today, they won't give back tomorrow—and they will eventually leave. Remember The Water Cycle Principle from Chapter Two in the context of the workplace? You already know that each participant must give more than he or she takes from the next cycle participant. As the leader, you may already understand that, but your people may not. So, beyond seeing, growing, and involving your talent, you must teach them to give first, too. Teaching them to give is the cornerstone secret to seeing them, growing them, and involving them.

We've said this before, but two things are required for human beings to feel fulfilled. One, humans must grow in all areas of their lives. Two, humans must give to others through their time, talent, and resources. If you only do one, you must give, because when you give, you grow. We already showed you in the "Grow Them" chapter how to grow your employees. That takes care of the first part of the fulfillment equation. This chapter takes care of the other part of the equation. Do both, and you'll be a source of fulfillment for your employees. They'll be hard-pressed to leave.

GIVING IS THE OPPOSITE OF TAKING

For too long, leaders have viewed employment as a "taking game." Employees take from their employers, and employers take from their employees. No wonder we have such high trust thresholds in our workplaces.

The opposite of taking is giving—giving to others and giving to yourself. When organizations take from everyone around them, they eventually run out of other people's stuff. But companies that provide never have a shortage of results.

Great companies give value first and give like crazy, period. They provide value to others first by helping them solve their problems. Because of that, they have no problem with getting a return on their investments. Employees who experience giving are more likely to give.

Many employees who move from a toxic work environment into a healthy environment don't adjust. They have created a defense shield around themselves to protect against the toxic environment. It is so close to them it becomes a part of them. Even when they leave the toxic workplace, they bring those same toxic habits into your organization. That is why you must teach your employees to give. Most individuals that work for you have not been encouraged to give at work. They come from workplaces that are brutishly competitive, hard-driving, and do not understand the power of purpose at work. If you don't show your new hires how your organization gives to each other and the customer, they will recreate the same toxic work environment they just escaped from. This time, they'll do it in your office!

Can you think back to the last time you helped someone? Maybe you gave to a charity, volunteered at a soup kitchen, or helped a neighbor who just went through surgery by mowing their lawn. Do you remember how you felt afterward? Incredible. Science shows the mental high after giving outranks the buzz after a pay raise.[5] In other words, it's entirely possible that giving is one of the most powerful fulfillment mechanisms. If you know that what you're doing is helping others, your life has meaning. If you like what helping others feels like, this chapter will show you how to teach your employees to feel the same way.

FOUR TYPES OF GIVING WITHIN COMPANIES

The American novelist and former president of Carnegie Corporation, John Gardner wrote:

"Wealth is not new. Neither is charity. But the idea of using private wealth imaginatively, constructively, and systematically to attack the fundamental problems of mankind is new."[6]

There are four perspectives on giving within companies. Each perspective is a mindset set by the leaders within the company.

1. It's the Company's Money, and They'll Give It to Whoever They Want.

Should companies give? It is an important question to ask if you want to keep your talent longer.

During the 20th century, academics and capitalists were defining the social role companies play in society. Was it enough to provide goods, services, and jobs, or should employers have a more prominent role in our world? And while many companies have self-regulated into a more philanthropic organization, others have been forced into changing after bad news. Think Nike's sweatshop-like work conditions and British Petroleum's (BP) environmental advocacy after the Deep Water Horizon oil spill.

Numerous studies show that corporate social responsibility is not only a good thing to do, but it increases profit as well. Researchers at Babson College reviewed more than 200 corporate social responsibility studies and found some incredible benefits of corporate giving. Companies who give back could increase the market value of the organization by at least six percent over 15 years. If companies have a public relationship with a charitable organization, the market value of the company grows 40 to 80 percent more than its competitors.[7]

Corporate giving increases trust. Customers and investors have more access than ever to the company's environmental impact and charitable contributions. Potential employees can choose organizations more aligned with their values. Investors and customers can support companies that represent their beliefs.

There is a problem, however, with the companies who give independently of their employees. We see it with companies seeking to retain young people all the time. They assume that it is enough to have a corporate social responsibility program. Wrong. You must give to the causes and efforts that are important to your people. Your giving must represent your values, your mission, and your people.

2. It's the Employees' Money, and They'll Give It to Whoever They Want.

Charity has a long history. Chinese classical thought taught the virtue of benevolence, although individuals in the Ming Dynasty gave secretly for fear of others considering their gifts politically motivated. Hindu writings exalted giving as an imperative duty. The ancient Greeks, African tribes, and even Native American history show a strong legacy of giving.[8] Philanthropy is often considered a moral or religious act.

When individuals give with this mindset, they see their charitable contributions as a personal choice. We conducted a national study on Millennials and giving. One of the things we measured was the type and frequency of gifts. Unsurprisingly, our results showed that Millennials want to give to projects that were local or international. It was either the local animal shelter or ending human trafficking. When we asked why they chose those organizations, the answer was simple. The causes were important to them, and they wanted to help make a difference.

Your employees should be encouraged to use their money to fix problems in society. They should be compensated in a way that they can still be charitable and generous towards others.

When individuals alone are expected to give, it misses the opportunity to engage some of the deepest passions that employees have. We walked Mary through *The PurposeFinder Formula*™ while she was experiencing a hard time at work. Mary is extremely passionate about human trafficking. Mary was a prosecuting attorney in Baltimore, working on some of the toughest cases you can imagine. Mary wasn't fulfilled. Her job was important. She made a difference every day. But, it was not the kind of change she was passionate about. Months later, Mary left her high profile position and moved to Los Angeles to raise awareness about human trafficking in Hollywood.

It is not enough to give as a company. It is not enough to empower your employees to give. You must discover how to tie the personal passions of the people that work for you to your company's charitable efforts.

3. Everyone Has Their Own Money, and No One Gives.

If you ask most people if they give to charity, they will say yes. When you ask when they gave their last charitable donation, things get quiet. That's because giving is down in the United States. According to a Giving USA report, the share of Americans who give money to charity fell from 68.5 percent in 2002 to 53.1 percent in 2016. Individuals, corporations, and foundations gave $410 billion in 2017 to nonprofits, faith-based organizations, and other charities. That marks a $20 billion increase from the year before, which is good news for nonprofits.[9] However, the upward corporate trend may not continue if individual giving continues to go down.

When individuals and companies refuse to give, no one wins. Individuals on the fringe of society who are unable to take care of themselves do not get the help they need. The charities addressing our most significant issues like homelessness and sex trafficking close down for lack of resources. Perhaps the most heartbreaking impact is when adults and children do not experience the joy of using what they have to help others.

4. Everyone Has a Say in Where We Give Together.

Walking into the light-filled southern California offices of Co.tribute, you can feel there is something different. It makes sense. Co.tribute is a tech company that empowers employees and vendors to participate in a company's philanthropy. After two decades, Philip Paul left his post leading major technology companies. He left to create a platform that would change the way companies think about giving—and it's working.

When you log into your Co.tribute account, you feel like you are on any other social media platform. You have friends, a story to scroll through, and plenty of pictures to distract you from work. What's different? You can utilize funds your employer deposits into your account to give to one of the hundreds of approved charities. It isn't just money. Co.tribute also allows you to purchase products for yourself that benefit a charitable cause. It could be a blanket that supports homeless shelters or serving plates made by the women of a remote African village.

Co.tribute eliminates the "black hole of giving," according to Paul Burke, the company's head of relationships. Most companies check the giving box once a year to receive tax benefits. They may enjoy the short-term benefits of tax relief but will miss out on the long-term impact of creating a culture built on giving back.

The only form of giving that will keep them longer is one where employees and companies work together to give back.

TO GET, YOU MUST GIVE

Teaching them to give is the last step of the Keep Them Longer method. It is also the most important. The "Teach Them to Give" principle is critical because it shows your employees what to do with what they have inside of them. Remember that Purpose is what you have inside of you to help others.

Let's say you do everything right. You invest by helping your employees find their purpose, grow them as whole people, and involve them in your community. You do all of that, but you don't show them how to do anything meaningful with it. You will see the money and time that you invested turn up void and the great habits you instilled atrophying before your eyes.

If you are not getting enough out of your employees, you are not giving enough to them.

"If it's not working out, I'll walk you to the door, give you a tissue, and not lose a wink of sleep over it," Shane said in his thick southern drawl. He let out his signature laugh at the end because even he knew how ridiculous it sounded. But Shane McCullar wasn't kidding. He meant every word.

When we called Shane, he was between sessions at an exclusive leadership conference in Austin, Texas. The tagline for the conference is, "The tribe for healthy, wealthy, generous men who choose to lead epic lives." It's fitting for the Tennessee native leading one of the fastest-growing Keller Williams Realty groups in the Mid-Atlantic.

Shane wants to be the best. He hates everything small: small paper clips, small offices, small thinking. Every time we sit down with him, somewhere in the conversation, Shane shares his goal: To be the #1 realty group in the state of Virginia. Right now, he's #5, but he's closing in fast. Shane doesn't just want to be the top guy in his industry. He wants to be the best person you'll ever work for. Shane said:

> "The biggest challenge is knowing that you'll only have them for a short period. It could be one year, five years, ten years. It's still a short period of time. This is a process, this is life, and this is part of their life. I want to be a highlight in their lives."

Shane started his realty group from scratch in 2007 and now has over 700 agents hitting $1.7 billion in volume this year. To grow that quickly, Shane had to learn what a healthy culture looked like. He had to develop processes and create an environment where his people felt trusted.

In a recent marketing meeting, Shane asked everyone to come prepared with three ideas. Everyone went around the room to share their thoughts until finally, Shane turned to one of the accountants and the lowest-ranked person in the room. Not expecting too much, but driven by his value of respect, Shane asked her what she had to share. The accountant proceeded to hand out materials for what she had drafted up. Impressed, Shane offered to give up his seat so she could present from the front of the room. She politely declined and proceeded to lead the group through a video and PowerPoint presentation from her place in the back. At the end of the meeting, Shane turned to his team, pointed at the accountant, and said, "She is in every meeting that relates to marketing from now on."

Shane gives it all to his employees. He is the last and final interview for every new hire. His voice is just as important as anyone else's. At any point in the interview process, a single interviewer can veto the decision to hire someone—whether they're the receptionist, an executive, or a manager. Because for Shane and his team, it is all about relationships.

"It all starts when you first get into a relationship with them," Shane said. His approach to keeping great people is to allow them to live out their purpose at work. Within the first interviews, his team is discovering what the company can do for the employees, not the other way around. Where do they want to be in life? How can this job get them there?

Giving becomes a core component of your culture when you create systems around it. You must make it a part of your core culture, written down, and addressed regularly. We asked Shane what his leadership pet peeves were. Immediately, he complained, "No one writes down their values or standards." The Keller Williams values are simple. God, Family, then Business. Organizations say that they care about people, but they don't have a program to support it.

They say they give back to the community, but there is no evidence of it in the office.

GIVING CREATES ACCOUNTABILITY IN BOTH DIRECTIONS

Giving is more than a day of service or an opportunity to share photos on social media. Giving is a core value. It is a habit. It is a solution to keeping them longer.

Giving is an essential step to keeping them longer. Here is how you teach someone how to give.

1. Giving Must Be Proportional to Their Talents.

A CEO may not be able to give time, but she can give money. A student may not be able to give money, but he can give time. The same is true within an organization. Individuals must be expected to give, but never expected to give the same way and in the same amount. Giving is a principle, not a scoreboard. Healthy organizations diversify their options to give and allow individuals to give in a way that works for them.

Giving requires sacrifice. Donating clothes that you don't wear anymore is not as satisfying as spending an afternoon at a soup kitchen. Teaching your employees to give means demonstrating what real giving looks like. It is not giving out of surplus; it is giving from a position of sacrifice.

2. Giving Must Utilize Employees' Purpose.

Michael Jr. is a comedian driven by purpose. When we sat down with Michael after his nearly sold-out show, he was still beaming. Michael is a professional comedian who doesn't live for laughs. He lives for what laughing does for people. Michael is funny. Very funny. On stage, his perfectly timed bits land seamlessly. Across the table at dinner, his eyes search the room for something to turn into material to make our group laugh. You would expect that of a Tonight Show and a Late, Late Show veteran. What you wouldn't expect? You wouldn't expect him to be so passionate about helping people find their purpose.

Michael tours the country hitting prestigious comedy clubs like Laugh Factory and The Comedy Store. Every time he does a show, Michael uses it as a platform to talk about purpose, which comes as an unexpected break from the observational-style humor of his jokes. Michael challenges his audience to serve others. But there's a catch. They can't use money. They have to use their talents. When we asked him why he challenges others not to use money, he said that people often give money to get out of getting their hands dirty. The way Michael sees it, the giver is missing out on the opportunity to watch a life transformation in front of their eyes.

You have to give with what's inside of you; your purpose. That's what giving is all about.

3. Giving Can Be Monetary or Nonmonetary.

Giving is not just monetary. It also includes how you spend your time, your attention, and your social capital.

Catchafire is a pro-bono volunteer platform. Started by Millennials unable to donate to their favorite charities, Catchafire pairs professionals with nonprofits in need. The platform empowers individuals to use their professional skills to help organizations they are passionate about. It isn't merely about using the skills people already have. Catchafire partners with companies to empower new or young employees to grow or diversify their skill sets.

Corporations like Viacom are creating their customized volunteer portal using the Catchafire platform. Viacom employees can sign up for pro-bono consulting calls, individual-based projects, brainstorming sessions, and live events that bring together nonprofits and Viacom employees. Viacom's Director of Social Responsibility Adam Robinson said:

> "It fills a need for the organization and helps that employee continue to sharpen that skill at the same time. It's about demystifying giving back and reminding our employees that having an impact should be fun, convenient, and, most importantly, rewarding."[10]

So far, Catchafire has matched over 5,000 nonprofits with 50,000 volunteers. The team continues to change the way individuals think about how companies and individuals can give back.

4. Giving Must Be Modeled.

If your parents gave or volunteered, you are more likely to do the same. Studies show that you are more likely to donate to the same type of organizations and volunteer in the same manner as your parents and your grandparents.[11] In short, modeling matters.

Leaders normalize behavior within an organization, whether good or bad. When they do, it permits others to adopt that behavior as well. If you want your team to be more giving, start modeling it. Remember the principle: "You must be what you want them to be." Ask if there is anything you can do for a colleague. Stay late to help someone else on their project. Buy lunch for the team and surprise them with their favorite entrees.

ESSENTIALS TO TEACHING THEM TO GIVE

Humans are designed to give. Our most fulfilling moments in life happen when we help someone else, even if it comes at great expense. Whether parenting, volunteering, or donating, all of these require giving your time or treasure to assist someone else. The final step of the Keep Them Longer method is to teach employees to give because it is the ultimate act of engagement. When you are giving, you are directly participating in the value flow described in The Water Cycle Principle. Most employees that come to work for you will not know how to give. It's not natural to them. Taking from one another is what employees and employers are used to. No wonder we have such toxic work cultures! Training your employees to give means demonstrating what giving looks like. If you give, you'll grow. If you never give, you'll never grow.

PART 3:
THE PROCESS
Say Goodbye to Expensive Turnover

GAIN THEM

On November 13, 2018, Amazon.com announced it would be opening up two new headquarters on the East Coast.

The announcement came after months of rumors circulated about which cities would be chosen. It was high drama—somewhere between picking the next Olympics host city and a new Pope.

Each new headquarters promised to create 25,000 new high-paying jobs plus 10,000 additional support jobs within the surrounding communities. The world went wild when the news broke that Arlington, Virginia and Queens, New York were selected. The $5 billion investment between the two locations would instantly benefit the surrounding economy, real estate market, and the education system.

"We are excited to build new headquarters..." said Jeff Bezos, Founder and CEO of Amazon.com, in their public announcement. "These two locations will allow us to attract world-class talent that will help us to continue inventing for customers for years to come. The team did a great job selecting these sites, and we look forward to becoming an even bigger part of these communities," said Bezos.[1]

Three months later, they would reverse their New York selection and make Northern Virginia the sole winner.[2] Do you know who wasn't excited about the online mammoth moving into their backyard? The local Northern Virginia employers.

They weren't worried about losing their customers. They were concerned about losing their employees. They should have been. There were reports of other companies set to relocate to Northern Virginia that reversed their plans for fear of a dried-up talent market. It wasn't just technology companies that were concerned. Nearly half of the 25,000 jobs were jobs outside of coding and traditional technology roles.[3]

Could your company or organization withstand a tech giant like Amazon.com moving into the neighborhood? Or, would your employees be looking for reasons to jump? Could your company attract talent away from a company like Amazon.com? Do you have what it takes to gain the best talent?

THE GREEN PASTURE EFFECT

Employees that are not being developed at their current companies fall victim to the "Green Pasture Effect," which drives high turnover—especially in competitive talent markets. However, the grass is greener where you water it. Watering your employees in the form of development is key to keeping them longer.

We're not talking about disgruntled employees here. We're talking about the talent that may be only slightly dissatisfied. Seventy-one percent of your employees are actively looking for another job right now.[4] If you are in one of the hundreds of markets dwarfed by a cadre of major employers, there is hope. Our research shows that the reality in working for some of these major brands isn't as shiny as it appears. And, if you work at a major brand, this is your wake-up call to make specific changes to improve culture and keep them longer.

LivingSocial is an excellent example of what not to do. The once-popular daily deal app (similar to Groupon.com) allowed customers to get specialized deals and significant discounts for products, services, and experiences. The LivingSocial headquarters in Washington, D.C. became a hotbed for new and fresh talent— and the facility reflected the fun culture that the app provided its customers.

In less than ten years, it had grown to be one of the District's largest employers. LivingSocial touted lots of fun plus free food, a ball pit, and even a rock wall. Walking into the LivingSocial headquarters, applicants and interviewees were met with a fantastic circus of fun at work. It's no wonder the modern coupon company had no problem gaining talent.

But LivingSocial couldn't keep them.

Despite having the façade of a fun culture, their actual culture was toxic. Former employees have admitted to us that the rock wall and midday yoga classes were cool, but they never felt empowered to do their work. For LivingSocial, bad leadership canceled out the cool stuff. The company shrank from a peak of 4,500 employees in 2011 to about 200 in 2016 from a combination of layoffs and turnover.[5] The LivingSocial headquarters sat vacant for years before being renovated and reused by another young app company. We're not sure if they kept the rock wall, but we certainly hope they learned the lesson of their former tenants. Culture first, rock wall second.

In short, your brand may gain people to work for you, but it may not keep them. In this chapter, we will show you how to hire to keep them longer.

FIND OUT WHY THEY WORK FOR YOU

One of the first things we do when designing a recruiting and onboarding program for clients is to determine why their current employees decided to work there in the first place. Was it a better commute? Did they love the opportunity for advancement? Were they attracted to the industry and the chance to learn something new?

Each of your employees has their own unique stories. They have their reasons for choosing your industry, joining your company, and coming to work for you day after day. Do you know what those reasons are?

Ask your team the following questions to determine why they chose your organization over your competitor. The answer to these questions should influence how you develop and implement your hiring strategy.

- What was the #1 deciding factor for why you chose to work here?
- Were you weighing multiple opportunities or options? If so, what were the factors that you were considering?
- What kind of research did you do about our company before getting hired?
- Why did you choose to leave your last job and join us?
- What were your expectations on your first day here? Did we meet, exceed, or destroy those expectations?
- What aspects of the hiring process made us more attractive to you?

Your employees' answers to these questions will help you recast your recruiting and onboarding experience. Plus, it will help you train your leadership on the language that defines your culture.

NEVER STOP RECRUITING THEM

When we got married, we received some great advice. We were told never to stop dating one another. As a couple, you understand the need to keep engaging the other person. Go out of your way to make the other person feel special. Plan a vacation once a year. Take turns planning a date night.

According to a national study on marriage, the main reasons that people cite for getting a divorce is a lack of commitment. Most people think that it's infidelity. It isn't.[6]

Anyone who has been in a committed relationship knows that it requires being intentional. Great marriages, like great corporate cultures, don't just happen. The principle of intentional engagement works within companies as well.

Every day that you lead your team, you are working to re-recruit them to stay. When you are recruiting new talent, you put your best foot forward. You highlight your generous benefits package. You introduce them to current employees who love working for you. You compliment their experience and affirm their choice.

Then comes the big proposal. You give the recruit an offer letter. You both agree on terms and enter into a working relationship. Then you stop pursuing them. You stop engaging and reminding them why they love working for you. You don't feature your benefits or do the activities that drew them to you initially. You may offer some basic professional development, but it's executed poorly.

Then fire fades. The employee calls it quits, and you wonder what happened. Human nature is consistent across the planes of our experience. We all crave intentional engagement, significance, and community. Employers who forget to engage their employees at all levels always will never keep them longer.

RECRUITING FOR RETENTION

Poor retention is often blamed on poor recruiting. Although you must indeed hire great people before you keep great people, the blame is unjust. The relationship between recruiting and retaining is synergistic. One cannot exist without the other. Hiring great people leads to great culture. Keeping great people leads to a steady flow of more great hires. People want to work at a great company. People also want to work where their friends work.

The first way to prevent turnover is to, of course, hire better. Recruiters and managers rarely work together to fill positions. Recruiters are told to go out into the world and bring back qualified candidates who can do a specific set of skills. They are handed a mediocre and overly general job description. Then those recruiters are then evaluated based on their ability to deliver an excellent fit for the job. The most effective recruiting happens, however, when the manager and the recruiter work closely together on the job description, necessary qualifications, and the culture fit.

The conversation around recruiting for retention should center around the Employee Compatibility Drivers. They are as follows:

- **Culture & Values** - Do recruits fundamentally align with the mission of the organization? Do recruits appreciate how you serve customers, what your priorities are, and where the company invests its money? Values are often communicated in a company's "triple-bottom-line": people, planet, profit. Values are becoming an increasingly popular topic brought up by a new generation of candidates in their first interview.

- **Work Ethic** - Do they have what it takes to get the work done? Asking situational interview questions helps (e.g., "Tell me of a time when you took on a project outside of your skillset?"), but behavioral questions are better (e.g., "What would you do if you were put in charge of a project that you did not have expertise in?"). The interview is the first step to setting expectations. We have public accounting clients whose employees drop like flies around tax time. That's even though new accountants were told the role includes late nights and working on the weekend!

- **Learned Skill Sets** - Can the recruits do the job with their current skill set, or will they require additional training to be effective in the role? This question is typically the first to come up, but it is only one of the six drivers you hire for. Résumés are becoming increasingly less reliable. That's why you need to ask questions around the solutions that they can provide in the role. You cannot ask candidates to give real advice to your company's current problems. Not asking for advice from recruits protects you from being accused of abusing the interview process to get free advice.

- **Adaptability and Teachability** - Do the recruits have what it takes to go with the flow? Are they willing to learn and take feedback well? Some employees are incredible producers but have a hard time adjusting to changing timelines or new information. Others are very ambitious but can't handle correction. Teachability is the most critical quality to hire for. You can develop skills within an individual, but you cannot teach someone to be teachable.

- **Drive** - How ambitious are they? Knowing where they see themselves in the future (without asking the age-old, "Where do you see yourself in five years?") is essential for projecting their advancement. It will also help inform how to equip the team to welcome them effectively. Ask questions around their expectations about moving up within the company and provide an example of a timeline that they would be proud of.

- **Ownership** - How important is it for them to have a say in how things turn out? Will they do what it takes to get the work done? Understanding what they think about employer versus employee responsibility is essential for hiring self-sufficient employees, as opposed to entitled ones.

YOUR BRAND IS A CRUCIAL RECRUITING TOOL

"We can't compete with these other brands."

We were speaking with a human resources director at a manufacturing site in a rural community in middle America. Qualified candidates were always hard to come by for her company, but with young employees moving to cities in droves, it seemed nearly impossible.

She isn't the first to share her frustration around employer brand. A mismanaged brand is just as dangerous to your customer success as it is to your candidate success. Employer brand matters beyond the updated logo and modern fonts. Your employer brand includes everything the candidate sees, feels, smells, and thinks about your brand.

Don't believe us? We are going to list some companies, agencies, and organizations in America and see how you react to their brand. Read their names and see what comes to mind:

- McDonald's
- Minneapolis Twins
- Apple
- Enron
- FBI
- Los Angeles Public Library
- Whole Foods
- The White House
- Walmart
- San Quentin Prison

Odds are, you had a specific reaction to each of these companies. Your mind may have brought up images of golden arches or modern white showrooms. Perhaps you considered your own experience with the brand. Did it give you good thoughts or bad thoughts?

Think about what kind of person works at each of the employers listed. Do you like who that person is? Would you want to spend time with them at a dinner party? Would you recommend them for a position in your company?

As soon as you say that you work at The White House—depending on who is currently occupying it—says a lot about who you are and what you believe. As soon as you say that you work at McDonald's, people have preconceived ideas about what your work looks like. Your company's brand impacts your entire hiring process. That is why you need to have a positive employer brand to recruit great people.

When it comes to gaining great talent, how recruits feel about what you do is just as important as what you do.

THREE COMPONENTS OF A GREAT EMPLOYER BRAND

1. Personality

You would never pursue a friendship with someone who has no personality, would you? Of course not. Your employees don't want to work at a company with no personality, either. Personality doesn't mean painting your walls bright orange and having dance parties every day at 3:55 p.m.

Personality means your company has a unique approach to solving problems. There needs to be something unique about who you are and how you do things. Your company's personality may include: how you evaluate problems, how you serve customers, how you treat employees, or how you deliver services.

Here is an activity to assess your employer personality. Write out a list of at least 15 unique characteristics your company possesses. This list may include everything from, "We are unafraid of asking the big questions" to, "We respect tradition and honor the best practices implemented by our founders." From those 15 characteristics, narrow it down to your top five employer personality traits. Those will then guide your branding and culture. The power of personality is that it is uniquely yours. This activity will help your recruiting team in selling the role to potential recruits and managers to keep them longer.

2. Personalization

A great employer brand gives employees the ability to personalize their experience. Nearly everything in our lives is personalized. Algorithms curate our playlists and our Netflix queue according to our preferences. In the same way, great employer brands give employees a say in how the company's personality is expressed. It must consist of every individual understanding and internalizing the big brand of the company. A key step to doing this is to help them understand their purpose and how to apply it at work (See Chapter 7 for how to do this).

When your employees feel personally connected to your brand, they are more likely to share their positive experiences with others.

3. Purpose

What is the purpose of the company? The purpose of your company is more than a mission statement, although we show you what goes into an effective mission statement in the last chapter. The purpose of your company is beyond what you do. It's why you do it. Help your customers, employees, and members of the community understand the driving force inspiring the company.

Purpose often comes from the Origin Story of the company. Some of the most prominent brands are formed and grown around the impactful story of the founder. Sara Blakely started Spanx because she couldn't find effective shapewear. William Boeing built a seaplane because the replacement parts for his recreational plane didn't come in. Larry Page started Google after writing a college paper on the structure of the world wide web. Rediscover the hole in the market that your company's founders were seeking to fill and share the story. Talk about the struggle and triumph with every candidate who comes through your doors.

WHAT ATTRACTS EMPLOYEES TO WORK FOR YOU

Through our research, we have determined that employees are attracted to work at a company for one of four reasons. For some employees, one of these reasons will rank higher than others, while other employees will weigh their ultimate decision between two or more of these factors:

1. ## Compensation – They Want a Higher Salary or Better Benefits.

"Of course, they're quitting! They want more money!"

Compensation comes in many forms. Most folks consider it wages and traditional benefits, but it can also include non-traditional elements like profit-share and ownership in the company.

We were speaking at a conference for chief nursing officers in Virginia. In one of our keynote sessions, we asked the attendees why they first became a nurse. We will never forget the honest answer of one woman. Her career choice came down to either nursing or bookkeeping. The only reason she chose nursing was that nursing paid slightly more! Her decision impacted every area of her life. She chose her life's career based on money. It affected where she would live, the type of coworkers she would have, and how she would meet her husband. Money was her primary motivator.

Most companies have been taught to pay their employees higher than their competitors, or else their staff will quit. In his book EntreLeadership, Dave Ramsay explains it clearly: "You have to pay your people well because salary translates to appreciation in the eyes of your team."[7]

It's true. Of course money matters. Our homes, cars, and smartphones all cost money. However, money isn't the only box that employees are looking to check when applying for jobs.

2. Brand - They Recognize the Brand, and the Brand Means Something to Them.

"That's so cool you work there!"

Every year, the National Society of High School Scholars does a national survey regarding the next generation's top choices for employers. Graduating high school seniors across the country are asked what companies they would like to work for when they graduate. The brands that make the list won't surprise you. They include Apple, Disney, Facebook, FBI, CIA, and others.[8] People are attracted to what they know. We certainly see this in big brands that we work with. Employees will be attracted to the brand first and the job description second.

For some brands, their reputation in the consumer market is their most significant asset. This is true even if their track record as an employer may not be great. Amazon.com is a perfect example. The online mogul is a brand that employees flock to from all over the world. However, their demanding and competitive culture makes the brand a target for high turnover.

But Amazon.com does not have a hiring problem. Why? Because even if the candidate knows that the workplace is less than ideal, they are willing to endure the experience to list the major brand on their résumés.

There are certainly benefits for working at a recognized brand. The brand intrigues people, and they want to know more about what you do and how you got the job. The brand becomes an instant validator for you and your experience. The brand becomes a part of your identity and can help improve your career prospects.

3. Opportunity – They Want to Advance Their Career, Obtain a New Skill Set, or Grow Professionally.

"I just want more opportunity."

Lack of opportunity is one of the top reasons that employees quit, but opportunity is a major reason that candidates apply. Through surveys and focus groups, we have found "opportunity" to have different meanings to different people. In a focus group in Northern Virginia, the respondents all agreed that opportunity was the ability to gain professional and personal development at work. While another focus group from the same company, this time with managers in the Midwest, yielded results that defined opportunity as the speed in which you advance.

Opportunity is both perception and reality. The leadership at a major car brand all listed opportunity as a major reason that they chose to work and stay working at the brand. At that same company, we asked new and young employees why they would quit. Respondents used the same word: opportunity.

How could it be that the same word that keeps one set of employees engaged also threatens to push out an entirely different employee population?

Organizations often lure new talent to work for them with the promise of opportunities to apply their skill sets, have access to more clients, or work with new industries. However, if the opportunity is not what it appears to be, employees are willing to move jobs and find actual opportunities elsewhere.

4. Lifestyle – They Want Work-Life Balance.

"I don't want to give up my life to work here."

Forty percent of U.S. employers offered paid maternity leave in 2018. That may not sound like enough (it isn't), but that is up 16 percent from 2015.[9] The nature of work and new maternity leave best practices have now allowed moms and dads to work and raise a family.

Lifestyle employees aren't just busy parents. They are also young creatives who want to travel while growing their career. They are men wanting to ditch the commute and women who prefer to work from a home office rather than a distracting central office.

Lifestyle employment is so popular that entire industries are being created around it. The gig economy allows workers to work when and how they want on an infinite number of projects. The lifestyle employee seeks trust and empowerment to get their work done on their terms. They do not thrive under micromanagement and are motivated by big goals and clear deadlines.

THE BIGGEST, BADDEST, AND MOST COMMON RECRUITING MISTAKES

Companies with significant retention issues rarely think to look at their recruiting process. That is a considerable mistake. Unfortunately, it isn't the only mistake they make.

Here are the five most common mistakes that leaders make when it comes to recruiting new talent.

1. Leaders Are Not Honest.

Out of all the mistakes, this is the most upsetting. When we survey a company to determine why their turnover is happening, we often discover that their best and brightest are leaving because of unkept promises. Can you blame them? If a manager provides a promotion timeline upon hiring, the employee has no reason not to trust them. When that timeline doesn't happen, good people leave.

It is better to be open and honest with your employees about their future. If you are dishonest, it may help you in the short term, but it will do severe damage in the long run. For example, if you have an employee who was promised a promotion within two years of being hired and that doesn't happen, they are at risk of quitting. If you don't have the position available, tell them. If they aren't ready for advancement yet, tell them. The solution is to redefine a path that fits their expectations and goals.

Even if they leave, they will not harbor bitterness or resentment. That's because you were honest.

2. Leaders Don't Provide a Timeline.

A great recruiter gives sample timelines for what this position will include and when. Employees today are eager to know what's next. They are curious about the road ahead, what their training schedule could consist of, and how long it takes to be proficient in the role.

It is important to provide examples rather than hypotheticals. Give them real-world scenarios of individuals within the role who have gone on to do great things. Share what the candidate needs to acquire in terms of skills and how long it will take them to become proficient. Real-world examples will help reset any unrealistic expectations and encourage an open conversation about career progression from day one.

3. Leaders Don't Ask the Right Questions.

Do you know the most compelling questions to ask in an interview? They aren't the standard questions you typically get trained to deliver. You will never hear us training clients on asking the infamous question, "What are your strengths and weaknesses?" Everyone is inclined to stretch the truth. Interviews are opportunities for both parties to vet the other.

For example, try asking, "Based on what you know about us as a company, how do you believe you can help us achieve our goals?"

This simple question gets to three fundamental elements of a great interview. First, you will learn how they prepared for the interview. Their answer will show you how serious they are about the job and how they get ready for important appointments. Second, it will show how they see their future role in the company. If they have an answer ready, they look at their role as a contributor to the team. If they don't have an answer, odds are they are not a self-starter or critical thinker. Third, this question determines if they are a giver or a taker. Are they more focused on what they can bring to the company or what the company can do for them?

4. Leaders Have Bad Job Descriptions.

If you get hundreds of applications for every job listing, listen up. In the world of online recruiting, candidates "Shoot, Point, Aim" instead of "Aim, Point, Shoot." They send off applications without reading the requirements and upload incorrect or poorly drafted résumés.

If you are using an online job board, your job description is your stop-gap against time-wasting applicants. The best job descriptions give clear and specific examples of what the job will include. Ditch the glittering generalities like "looking for a team player who is committed to excellence" and opt for something that points to what the employee will be doing.

Include "Easter Eggs," small mysteries included in the job description that only serious applicants will notice. That could include asking them to upload a résumé video, write their name in the subject line, or connect with you on LinkedIn.

5. Leaders Make It All About Them.

This error is the most common mistake companies make when hiring. Companies who are more focused on filling a role than bringing in a new team member make it all about them. They should be asking about the candidate and determining if they are a good fit.

Here is the foundational principle for retention: Make it about them, and they'll make it about you.

We were working with a multi-level-marketing client who was having a hard time reaching Millennials. We were brought in to work with some of the top performers to deliver a solution that would be implemented across the company. What we found was so simple, it was shocking. When the company was recruiting new members, they continued to use the mantra, "Join us." It was even a hashtag.

Now, this was a great company with a great mission. However, their mindset was all wrong. They made it all about who the company was and nothing about what the individual brought to the table. Companies need to shift their mindset from "You were nothing before us" to "You were someone before us; that's why we want you."

HOW TO NEVER HAVE A HIRING PROBLEM

Wouldn't it be amazing not to have a hiring problem ever again? It is possible, and we will show you how below. Companies that don't have recruiting problems have three things in common.

1. Big Ideas

People are drawn to the impossible, the improbable, and the incredible. When someone says where they work, they want the other person to be impressed, or at least intrigued. Companies that don't have hiring problems utilize their affinity for big, scary, crazy ideas to be the honey that draws candidates to them.

2. Big Brands

The bigger the name, the more attractive it is to a candidate. Not just because of the immediate cool factor of working for the company. A major brand on a résumé is an incredible asset in a competitive job market. Big brands often bank on this, knowing that they can rely on their name and skimp on the culture. But other big brands utilize their corporate goodwill and find the best and brightest from around the world.

3. Big Vision

It isn't just a big vision that works. You must have a clear vision as well. The more you communicate with your employees and your recruits what problem in the world you are seeking to solve, the easier it will be to fill job openings.

ESSENTIALS TO GAIN THEM

Keeping them longer starts with hiring them smarter. Companies with retention challenges often blame recruiters for not finding quality candidates. They never reflect on how they can build a better hiring process. Companies that keep them longer pair up recruiters, managers, and team members to evaluate recruits.

Great companies intentionally build their hiring process to discover the "character fit" of the candidate, not just the "skill fit." One of the best strategies for attracting great people is to define a clear employer brand that reflects your corporate values. The next step is to ask the right questions. Asking the right questions ensures that you are bringing on the right people—people who are committed to personal and professional transformation.

HOW TO DO THIS

- **Discover Why They Chose To Work For You** - Issue a survey to your employees and discover what inspired them to choose to work for you over a competitor. Use this to build your retention strategy (do more of the stuff that keeps them), as well as to recruit great people to your team (feature the things your employees love).

- **Write Better Job Descriptions** - Job descriptions are the window dressing of your recruiting efforts. How you showcase the opportunity will determine the quality of candidate you receive. Work with the team who will be working with the new hire to create an accurate and aspirational job description.

- **Build A Better Brand** - You inherit what you attract. Your corporate brand will either attract great people to work for you or discourage great people from ever applying. Evaluate how well your brand reflects your values and list your top 5 values.

- **Never Stop Recruiting Them** - Recruiting goes beyond the hiring process. Recruiting that leads to retention must include continuous engagement reminding employees why they love working for you.

14

TRAIN THEM

"The key to retaining talent is promising and then delivering growth." **–Brian Bencz, Vice President of Land Development at Lennar**

Nancy Agee is one of the most powerful female healthcare executives in the country. As a child, Nancy endured a cancer scare that lasted two years, included five surgeries, and landed her in a wheelchair. Although her diagnosis proved to be temporary, the experience she had as a patient in a Southwest Virginia hospital inspired her to pursue a career in healthcare.

Nancy is known as the candy striper who made her way to the C-suite of Carilion Clinic.[1] Her corner office is light-filled and on the fourth floor of one of the hospital buildings. It overlooks a construction site where Virginia Tech, in partnership with Carilion, is building out their newest nurse training facility.

Nancy is passionate about education.

"In the way back, having more education meant you had more job opportunities. Now training is the intellectual conversations that create more collaboration," she said.

Nancy views training in the appropriate context. The supportive resources her hospital system provides to its medical staff are only as useful as the application. But Nancy is the kind of leader that admits they need to improve continuously. Her biggest training need is helping people work together and understand where each other are coming from.

Every time you speak to Nancy, she references a recent conversation with someone who is a young employee or mom re-entering the workforce. As a beneficiary of mentoring, Nancy has made an effort to send the elevator back down. Mentoring is important in a high-turnover, high-stakes career such as nursing.

When we sat down, Nancy had just talked to a young woman who wanted to switch jobs because she didn't like to work late. This young nurse voiced her concerns and desires to her manager and was rotated to another unit with different hours. The average time a nurse stays in his or her role is seven years. A hospital system like Nancy's is prepared for the turnover. So Carilion embraces internal rotation because it means people aren't getting burned out. That's good for nurses and patients alike.

What's the key, according to Nancy? There must be an environment in which people can voice their concerns. Managers must be trained in coaching their employees, not merely supervising. If employees aren't enjoying their work, they will look for other opportunities. They must receive training in the skills that can take them to new opportunities within the organization. That kind of training leads to internal transfers and positive turnover. Positive turnover occurs when someone leaves to further their goals or dreams.

TRAINING LIES, LEADERS LOVE

What you believe about training will determine how you train your people. Do you think that it is your responsibility to train your employees, or your employees' responsibility to get the training they need? We have found this question to be one of the most informative in measuring a development program. Not understanding the responsibility around training is one of the challenges companies face. There are four myths that leaders believe about training that prevent them from keeping talent longer:

1. "They should already be trained."

For employers that hire for skills and not character, this is their core belief. "It's not our responsibility," they say, "That's why they went to college." But companies that only evaluate what their recruits know before their first day on the job are missing out. They're missing out on what they'll be able to do in the future with effective professional development. It's more affordable to train someone than to replace them.

2. "They will leave anyway, so why spend the money?"

The existence of professional development opportunities is a key factor as to whether or not an employee chooses to stay. According to one report, Millennials cited a lack of training and development opportunities as a big reason they were leaving companies.[2] Investing in your people doesn't have to be expensive, but it does have to be intentional. Training every person on your team as a whole person shows them that they matter and that their contribution is consequential.

3. "What's worked before will work today."

Retro may be cool for interior design, music, and fashion, but it does not work for employee development. The way we learn today is different than how we learned twenty or thirty years ago. From how we access new information to how we demonstrate what we know, the world of development has evolved. Your training program must evolve as well.

4. "Even the best training cannot replace experience."

Experience matters. No one wants to be a surgeon's first procedure, a pilot's first passenger, or a dentist's first extraction. We trust people with years on the job. However, practical training can help shorten the curve between starting a job and becoming an expert in a skill or craft.

HOW WE LEARN

The human brain is made up of 100 billion neurons. These brain cells form an incredibly intricate system called the neural network. The fascinating thing about this neural network is that it can be changed. Every time we learn something new, a new tiny "branch" forms in our minds. That branch forms faster and is stronger when it is connected to an existing neuron. That is why a guitarist can learn to play the ukulele faster than someone who has never played an instrument at all. A synaptic connection occurs when the brain is processing, questioning, and then connecting that new information to an existing memory or dataset. [3]

We learn more when the information can build on top of the experiences we already have. Brain scientists have been able to track the growth of these small branches and see how they grow when there is consistent training.[4]

To protect the investment of corporate training, organizations should opt for more engaging activities such as discussion groups and task forces focused on solving problems. They should avoid lectures and video-heavy programs: the more stimuli, the more learning. With better-designed education, changes occur within organizations. Employees replace bad habits and harmful mindsets with new, positive ones. We know that adults and children learn differently. Within many organizations today, training employees mimic the elementary classrooms that they left decades earlier.

Malcolm Knowles helped bring the concept of Adult Learning Theory to America at the end of World War II. A contemporary and friend of Merriam Webster, Malcolm developed a method for how adults learned called "andragogy."

1. **Adults Need to Know Why** - Adults need to know the reason for learning something.
2. **Experience Is the Foundation of Learning** - Both positive and negative experiences create learning in the brain.
3. **Buy-In** - Adults need to be involved in the development and delivery of their education.
4. **Relevance** - Adults are most interested in learning subjects that have an immediate connection to their work and personal lives.
5. **Problem Solvers** - Adult learning focuses on solving problems rather than processing content.
6. **Motivation** - Adults respond better to internal versus external motivators.[5]

WHOLE PERSON TRAINING

Whole Person Training is a new way of training. It provides a comprehensive solution to high turnover as it addresses the six core elements impacting turnover. Whole Person Training is revolutionary because it addresses the multi-dimensional needs of your employees. Some organizations readily believe that providing Whole Person Training will benefit their overall culture. Others have a hard time seeing the need to train their employees on "non-essential" skills.

Whole Person Training includes these core elements:

1. Compliance

First (this should be a given), you must train your employees on the "rules, regs, and matters of compliance." This training should include your employee handbook (which should be digital by now) and training on matters of sexual harassment, diversity, safety, etc.

Your compliance training is typically designed to be presented one-on-one or in a classroom setting. Consider creating a digital version so that your employees can reference it at a later date. You may also want to design interactive compliance training. For example, leverage video or interactive training to present information on the health benefits you provide. Have them create a scenario for how they would utilize the benefits. Then, have them ask questions or look through the resources to come up with a solution.

Compliance Courses Include:

- OSHA Training
- Cyber Security Best Practices
- Respect Training
- Anti-Harassment Training
- Workplace Violence Training
- Diversity and Inclusion
- Unconscious Bias Training

Consider what compliance training is most appropriate for your organization. You may currently offer great compliance content, but you may need to adjust how it is delivered.

2. Mastery

Show your employees how to work better. Yes, you hired them because they had specific qualifications and core competencies, but learning should never stop. That's especially true given that the two things that contribute most to human happiness and fulfillment are growth and giving. You might have sales employees that are great at their current jobs. Consider how to provide training that increases their mastery and expands their responsibilities.

Mastery training improves employees' confidence, effectiveness, and execution. Mastery training most often includes industry-recognized certifications and continuing education (CE) credits. Industry associations or related groups offer these courses. Many universities provide ongoing professional development training, both online and in person. You may also provide mastery training by internal trainers with relevant expertise. The key to offering mastery training is to carefully connect the program to the professional goals of the individual employee. Arbitrary or poorly communicated mastery training requirements do not correlate to high retention.

Mastery Courses Include:

- Certified Public Accountant
- SHRM-CP
- Certified Management Accountant

- Facebook Ads; Google AdWords Training
- Design Driven Innovation
- Program Management

The mastery courses that you offer or reimburse must correlate to the current trajectory of the employee. Provide sample mastery course offerings as well as encourage employees to seek out relevant courses.

3. Communication

Your employees need to be empowered with the skills to communicate with others. Empowerment is essential for every employee in every position. Providing relevant communication training will equip your employees with the confidence to share their vision while working with colleagues and clients alike.

Communication Courses Include:

- How to Give and Receive Feedback
- Conflict Resolution
- Mastering Online Communications
- LinkedIn Personal Branding
- Defining Communication Expectations
- Persuasive Selling
- Effective Presentations

Identify core communication challenges faced by your employees and offer ongoing training. Communication courses are best delivered regularly and in short formats to ensure habit formation.

4. Leadership

Start training your employees to lead. Leadership development has been a staple of employee training. Unfortunately, most leaders force employees to prove themselves before being trained as a leader—rather than giving them the leadership skills they need now. Leadership training should be proportionate to their experience and responsibilities. Offering relevant leadership training skills to employees shows that you are invested in their personal and professional development. It also opens the door to a more affordable and reliable leadership pipeline.

Leadership training should be provided to employees at every level of the organization. Organizations cannot wait to train someone to be a leader after they have been promoted. Provide leadership training opportunities that are appropriate and accessible to employees throughout their employee experience. The most effective leadership training is designed to develop the employee throughout their career.

Leadership Courses Include:

- Generational Leadership
- Managing Up
- Managing Remote Teams
- Personal Leadership Mastery
- Mentoring
- Coaching vs. Managing
- Becoming a Culture That Takes Responsibility
- Leading a Diverse Team

Design a leadership training program that equips employees with skills to lead themselves as well as lead others.

5. Personal Success

Today's employees view their work and life as integrated. Therefore, you must grow your people as whole people. In other words, show them how to live better. Through online and gamified training, teach them things like physical, nutritional, mental, relational, and financial wellness. The more stable they are in terms of personal wellness, the more stable they'll be at work. In fact, according to a Colonial Life study, more than 20 percent of employees spend at least five hours per week thinking about life stressors during work hours.[6] Stress at home breeds stress at work, and stress at work breeds stress at home. It's a nasty cycle. Personal wellness decreases stress and increases productivity and profitability.

Personal success is perhaps the most non-traditional form of training. It is designed to empower employees to have healthy personal and professional lives. Personal success courses increase engagement and loyalty while decreasing attrition and absenteeism.

Personal Success Courses Include:

- Personal Finance
- Finding and Applying Purpose
- Time Management Skills
- Goal Setting
- English as a Second Language

- Relationship Success Skills
- Emotional Intelligence
- Assertiveness Training

Personal success courses can be offered regularly to your team. Personal success programs are typically role and industry agnostic. You may want to offer them in person with included access to on-demand information and resources online.

6. Cross-Training

Cross-training includes courses and skills training that is unrelated to an employee's current role. Cross-training allows your employees to explore other passions they have or improve specific skills they are not currently exercising on the job. It also includes exposing employees to other aspects of your company. For example, an outgoing individual in the accounting department may be cross-trained in human resources. The key to practical cross-training is to encourage your employees to use their new skills at your company.

Cross-Training Courses Include:

- Adventure Photography
- Graphic Design
- Business Development
- Event Coordination
- Job Rotation
- Coaching Certification

Cross-training is the most flexible form of Whole Person Training. It may include exposing an employee to another department or sending them back to school. This is to be personalized by the employees. Consider what type of cross-training would best benefit your current employees.

TRAINING ALIGNED WITH VALUES

Horace said:

"I think it is key that we can capture new, fresh ideas— new ways of thinking and a new sense of values. We can translate that into being a better company with better service to our customers."

Horace Porras is one of those guys who you could listen to for hours. The American Tower Vice President of Human Resources has a story for nearly every scenario, which makes sense. Horace is responsible for growing and keeping American Tower's talent across Latin America. When you ask Horace what he does, he never has the same answer. He will start talking about connecting communities, working with Best Buddies International, or supporting a team of sustainability innovators. Maybe that's just what he's accomplished by our noon call.

Horace gets people, which is an excellent trait to have as the executive in charge of people. He advocates for hiring, training, and retention programs that lead to long-term habit changes. Because for Horace and his team, everything is based on value. When the priorities of the employer and employees are aligned, habits form faster.

"Everyone can add value," Horace said in his melodic accent. "We need to provide an experience. The employee needs to feel that he or she has a purpose. That the company is aligned with his or her values," he said.

When they are, creating a culture that runs on its own is easy. However, most companies don't know what their values are, let alone the values that they are hiring for. That's why training for American Tower starts at the interview process. Horace said:

"You have to state what the role actually does clearly. What are the deliverables? What is life like for that employee in that position? You must ask, 'Where will this employee perform at his or her maximum?' Every person performs at their best when they do what they love. They usually perform well at what they love because they have a purpose."

DESIGNING YOUR TRAINING PROGRAM

So how do you know if your training program needs to be updated? If you haven't updated your training program in the past five years, upgrading your training must be a top priority.

What does a remarkable training program include? Not all organizations can afford a video game-inspired training solution. They may not be able to change everything all at once. Or worse, they may use the excuse that because they can't make the ideal change, then they don't need to make a change at all.

That's like saying you won't order a salad for lunch today because tomorrow is Thanksgiving and you'll be eating heavier than usual. Every substantial improvement starts with an even more critical first step.

To evaluate how well your organization is doing, use the following checklist.

1. Is Your Training Creative?

Is your training process unique to the organization? The most effective programs engage multiple parts of the employees' brains. The best programs go beyond the typical classroom-style orientation. They should showcase your personality along with the unique challenges, character, and industry of your company.

2. Do Your Employees Regularly Review Your Training?

Do you ask for feedback from your employees as they go through the program? The only way you will discover how to improve your training is by asking your employees what they want, what they need, and how they need it.

3. Is Your Training Tied To Performance?

Is your training designed for maximum output? Your training is more than just developing your employees. When done correctly, your training will lead to higher revenues, more engagement, and happier customers. Develop metrics that track how the company makes or saves money, and you will have more buy-in for future improvements.

4. Is Your Training Flexible?

Is your training designed to change? Most training programs are created out of concrete. When new information or best practices are discovered, the old training needs to be uprooted entirely. We've all seen the cheesy corporate training videos from the 1990s and early 2000s. It's hard to take a company seriously when they don't seem to value training enough to make it relevant. Excellent training programs are designed to be updated regularly, both in content and delivery.

5. Is Your Training Personalized?

Does your training fit the needs, desires, and passions of the person being hired? Every person on your team is unique. They deserve an opportunity to customize their professional development. Great programs allow individual employees to design their career journeys within the company.

6. Is Your Training Experience-Driven?

Are your employees able to interact with the materials? More than simply reviewing the information, your employees must be able to understand and apply the knowledge. Experience-driven training is proven to be more effective than classroom lectures. Create programs that allow employees to learn and use the information immediately.

7. Does Your Training Include Both Individual Work And Group Interaction?

Is your training dynamic enough to work for both individuals and groups? Most organizations deliver training as either one-on-one sessions or group training. The best programs are designed to work both for individuals and groups. Consider how your education affirms how the individuals work within the organization.

8. Does Your Training Have An Immediate Application?

Is your training theory-based or application-based? The training that you provide must have an immediate application. Equipping employees for future situations is essential. However, most companies prepare their employees for situations that are so far in the future that the information is irrelevant. Create opportunities for learning where they can take and use the information immediately, even if that includes creating a manufactured scenario for them to practice the principles.

9. Is Your Training Designed To Create Habit Change Through Micro-Learning?

Is your training more focused on getting the information distributed or on creating change within the organization? Create training and growth tracks that deliver small packages of data over time rather than all at once.

10. Does Your Training Reflect Your Values?

Does your training introduce, affirm, and demonstrate your values? Training programs must showcase your values through stories and examples. Value-driven training is essential for keeping them longer.

ESSENTIALS TO TRAIN THEM BETTER

Developing employees is the responsibility of the leader. No one will know how to better equip them to serve customers, work together, and add value better than you, the employer. Unfortunately, there are limiting beliefs that leaders embrace that ultimately push responsibility of development back on the employee. Learning happens with or without training. The best training is hands-on and incredibly practical. Traditional classroom-style training will slow or even stall your employees' professional development. The most effective training programs equip the whole person and include compliance, personal success, professional mastery, communication, leadership, and cross-training. Your people are developing good habits because of positive inputs or they are forming bad habits because of negative inputs. How you design and implement your training will determine if you keep them longer.

HOW TO DO THIS

- **Review Your Current Training Options** - Survey current employees on the types of training that they would like provided. This can be done via anonymous survey as part of your scheduled engagement survey or one-on-one interviews.

- **Offer Whole Person Training Programs** - Great training starts with equipping employees to live and work better. Offer training that covers the six core elements of whole person training. If you cannot offer training internally, consider paying for online courses or hosting "lunch and learns" on topics such as financial wellness, relationship health, and communication best practices.

- **Design Your Program As Micro-Learning Modules** - Don't overwhelm your employees with information. Instead, offer mini courses on key topics that instill good habits over time.

- **Invest In Your Managers** - Consider how you equip your middle-managers. Are you giving them the kind of attention and development that they deserve? Remember that direct managers are the top reason employees quit. Equip those managers to keep them longer.

15

RETAIN THEM

The late Tony Schwartz is best known for the famous "Daisy Commercial" in the 1964 presidential campaign between incumbent President, Lyndon Johnson, and then-Senator Barry Goldwater.

Tony was also a branding expert behind brands like Alka-Seltzer and Coca-Cola.[1] Tony revolutionized the way that advertisers worked. Rather than taking the approach his contemporaries were taking in big New York ad houses, Tony did something else. Tony decided to look deeply into what people wanted and sell them what they already were thinking about. It is easier to convince someone that an ice-cold Coke would be refreshing if you know what a consumer thinks about when they're thirsty.

Reflecting on his political advertising career in a 1984 PBS documentary, Tony said, "There are four ways people can vote, for or against either candidate."[2] It isn't just politicians who divide your decision between "for" or "against."

When an employee considers leaving their company for another company, they have four choices. One, an employee can choose to stay with their current company because they like their job. Two, they can remain at their current company because they don't like the other opportunity. Three, they can choose to leave their current company because they aren't getting what they want. Four, an employee can leave and go with the other employer because it is a better opportunity. Ideally, the best leaders strive for their employees to make the first choice every day.

So, what are the core reasons why employees quit?

WHY EMPLOYEES QUIT

1. Leadership

The number one reason employees quit has to do with the relationship they have with their supervisors.[3] Plain and simple. At least 58 percent of workers say they'd take a job with a lower salary if that meant working for a great boss.[4] Gallup's Chief Scientist of Workplace Management and Well-Being, Dr. Jim Harter, admits that a manager influences 75 percent of what causes employees to leave. Employees can love their work, but if they hate their boss, they will still quit.[5]

Think about your own work experience. Do you have a favorite boss? What did you like about their leadership style? If we're guessing, it was how they inspired you, pushed you, and empowered you to become a better version of yourself. Even if the work was frustrating, a good boss could help you push through.

Now think about your least favorite boss. What made him or her so difficult to work for? Perhaps they lacked ethics or standards. Maybe they micromanaged around every turn. Perhaps they told you one thing and did another. Even if the work itself was fun, you still hated the situation.

Now think about you. Your leadership style is either keeping your employees longer or driving them away faster. How do you determine if your leadership style is dangerous? Ask the following questions of your employees in person or through an anonymous survey:

- Do you believe your manager has your best interests at heart?
- Do you trust your manager?
- Do you believe your manager will do the right thing, no matter the situation?
- Does your manager's leadership style help you do your job better?
- Does your manager support your professional goals?
- Do you feel a personal connection with your manager?
- Do you believe the team trusts your manager?
- Do you believe your manager's leadership style is well suited for the team?
- How can your manager improve how they lead the team?

To determine your leadership style, read the final chapter on Tools for Leaders.

2. Expectations

The connection between expectations and retention is one of the most useful conclusions our research has revealed. We all have expectations in our relationships. Sometimes those expectations are reasonable and healthy. Sometimes they are unrealistic and inappropriate. Other times the expectations aren't good or bad, but when they are never discussed, they can become dangerous.

Unspoken expectations are the most problematic.

If you're in a romantic relationship right now, you have both healthy and unhealthy expectations of your partner. For example, you expect them to love you back and treat you respectfully. If you are going on a date, you expect them to let you know if they'll be late. If you share finances, you expect them to discuss buying a new car. Those are healthy expectations.

But you may have expectations that aren't realistic. We have a friend who expected her husband to plan their summer vacation because her dad scheduled their family trip every year. The first big fight of their marriage started when she asked where they were going on vacation and what weeks she should request off work. Her husband looked like a freshman who forgot there was a test. Was he supposed to plan a vacation? Had they talked about this? Like any good husband, he never admitted to the fact that he had no idea what she was talking about. One week later, her husband told her that he had no idea he was supposed to plan the summer vacation. Our friend had never set expectations as to who was responsible for vacation planning. She assumed that her husband knew her wishes.

Employees have their own expectations, realistic and unrealistic. It's essential to determine what those expectations are, correct the bad ones, and fortify the good ones.

As discussed earlier, when we onboard a new employee, we ask them to write out their top three expectations for working with us. These could include their professional development schedule, compensation, access to clients, or level of responsibility.

Then, we write out our three expectations for them, which are the same for all of our team members.

- Think and act like the company is yours because it is.
- Serve our clients like longtime friends and treat your teammates like they're your family.
- Commit to your personal growth, don't take yourself too seriously, and be honest about your ideas, dreams, and concerns.

Then we come together to discuss and determine whether or not they are realistic, appropriate, and healthy.

We do this for several reasons. First, none of us are mind readers. We don't make assumptions about anyone's goals. We need them to share their thoughts, dreams, and concerns with us. Second, we want them to know that we have high expectations. An employee that feels trusted will work harder and more passionately than an employee who doesn't feel trusted. Finally, we want a baseline for feedback in the future. If an employee isn't meeting our expectations, we will go back to our expectations document and ask, "Are we both living up to our agreement?"

Your employees will quit if their expectations aren't met. Those expectations fall into four categories:

- **Compensation** - How much will they be paid now and in the future? How often can they expect a raise or a bonus? What can they expect to make in two years, five years, and ten years?
- **Responsibility** - What kind of decision-making power will they have now and in the future? How can they prove they are ready for a promotion? What does "ownership" look like, and how is it rewarded?
- **Lifestyle** - How will work intersect with their personal life? What does work-life balance look like for their role? What are the examples of people who work from home, have taken time off to raise a family, or leveraged flexible work hours?
- **Development** - Will they be given a mentor, or should they look for one themselves? Is there a budget for professional development? What can they expect to learn and be proficient in their first year on the job?

Expectations can make or break an employment relationship

3. Unclear Purpose

"Does what I do matter?" Every person on the planet wants to know the answer to this question. Employees that have an unclear sense of their purpose are at risk of leaving.

One of Gabrielle's mentors used to tell the story of two bricklayers. They were both asked what they were doing by a man who was walking by. The first stood up from the wall he was building and answered, "I'm laying bricks." The second bricklayer who was further down was asked the same. He picked up the next brick and, without hesitation, answered, "I'm building a cathedral." Both of these bricklayers were accurate, but only one had a purpose.

Every employee at every level of your organization wants to know two things. First, does their work matter? Second, how does their work matter? Unfortunately, most leaders assume the employees already know or will figure it out themselves. But your employees are looking to you to attach significance to their work.

We have had the opportunity to work with the military for the last seven years on engagement and retention strategies. We have learned a great deal from the decorated generals and leaders that we support. We can still remember a conversation with the base commander of a mid-Atlantic naval base. We were discussing the ongoing challenge of connecting the everyday work of his men and women to the mission of the Navy.

The official mission of the United States Navy is to maintain, train, and equip combat-ready Naval forces capable of winning wars, deterring aggression, and maintaining freedom of the seas. Though that sounds impressive, it isn't personal. If you ask a seaman what they're doing, their answer isn't going to be, "I am equipping combat-ready Naval forces capable of winning wars, deterring aggression, and maintaining freedom of the seas."

This base commander saw that the men and women on the base were losing their sense of mission, and he needed to light the fire and remind them of their purpose.

He did something pretty incredible. He started taking teams of people off-base to the shipyard and gave them a tour of the ships they were supporting. Most of them had never been on anything that big. He went through each part of the ship, sharing how it's used and why it was essential to the mission. He told stories of how the ships had helped humanitarian, peacekeeping, and combat efforts around the world.

He then had each person touch a part of the ship and think about how their daily work helped to support that big hunk of metal. Maybe one of the employees was in human resources and helped staff the base. Perhaps they were in technical support or training or catering. Every person had to articulate to their peers how their work supported that ship. As a result, you know what happened? The culture changed. People started seeing the mission behind their daily grind.

Every person, from the janitor to the CEO, needs to know that their work matters. Here's how to help employees find their purpose at work:

- Lead employees through *The PurposeFinder Formula*™.
- Connect their personal mission to the mission of the organization.
- Have employees interview clients and customers who have benefited from the work you do.
- Train managers and leaders to coach their teams from a place of purpose.

4. Unclear Career Path

Knowing what's next is key to finding stability and fulfillment in any career. If an employee is unsure about their next position and how they'll get there, they will seek opportunities that can offer that clarity. Thirty-two percent of employees quit because their current employer does not provide them the right career opportunities.[6]

We have worked with some of the world's largest brands to reduce their expensive turnover. In one engagement survey, we interviewed a young woman who had joined a major communications company six months earlier. She was in her mid-twenties, and the rest of her team were thirty-year veterans of the company. She enjoyed the wisdom and experience of the team. So we asked her what she loves about her job and what she would change. She rattled off the typical challenges that employees deal with: technology, work-life balance, and feeling overworked.

But then we tried a different question. We asked why this young woman would leave and go to work for another company. Bosses get nervous when we admit to asking their employees why they would quit. But wouldn't a good leader want to know so they could stop it? Knowing is better than being surprised when the employee decides to leave. Without hesitation, the young woman said:

> "I'm not sure where my career goes from here. There aren't any open positions in my department, and I just don't see what's next. The rest of my team has been in the same position for decades. I think I want something more exciting than that."

If this young woman was ready and willing to share her concerns with us, you better believe she told her friends and family about her frustration. If this company didn't make changes after our conversation with her, we're willing to bet she left for another opportunity or soon will.

You see, most organizations are set up to move slowly. That can be a good thing. But sometimes a slow pace can hurt your most ambitious employees. We know what you're thinking, "But they have to do it for years to become proficient. No one becomes an expert overnight!" We couldn't agree more. But companies need to measure talent, not timelines. Too many organizations rely on outdated, arbitrary promotion schedules, and it's hurting their bottom line. It all depends on how well you develop your people at each level. A more focused and streamlined approach to development will yield more impressive results. Don't get hung up on timelines.

It doesn't matter if you poorly train someone for two years or ten years. They're still poorly trained. If you have a plan that gives clear guidelines and expectations throughout an employee's career, you will be amazed at how quickly a driven person can grow. Your people want development. They want a challenge. They want to increase their abilities year over year. They want to know what their future looks like, and they want to be on a path that takes them there.

5. Lack of Training

They say that our ears and noses never stop growing. That may be true, but it isn't the only part of the human body that should continue growing. Our minds and our skill sets must always be improving, changing, and adapting to the world around us.

When employees know their company cares about their personal and professional growth, they want to stay longer. Every person wants to know that their company cares about their success. Some companies reserve professional development for high-performing or high-potential employees. But what kind of message does that send to the rest of the team?

Are they not "high-performing" enough? What is wrong with them that they aren't worth investing in? Training and development budgets are among the first to get cut when the economy drops. However, slashing professional development will hurt your ability to keep them longer.

The expense of developing your employees is far less than the cost of replacing them. There are cost-efficient ways to develop your employees. Not every company can or should send employees to professional conferences. Some of these events are incredibly powerful and can be the difference between keeping and losing your talent. Other conferences are a waste of time and money. Smart leaders invest in programs that equip their employees with skills to succeed in their job and life.

Most leaders are never taught to lead with their employees' needs in mind. How do you know what they need? To determine the training your organization should offer, ask the following questions of employees:

- What training or resources would help you do your job better?
- If you could get certified or professionally developed in one thing, what would it be?
- What additional training do you think your colleagues would most benefit from?
- What training currently offered do you think is a waste of time and resources?
- What additional training do you think your leaders need more of?

WHY EMPLOYEES STAY

Why employees stay is different than why they leave. Organizations that only focus on keeping them from quitting only get half of the equation right. True prevention is doing more of the good, not just avoiding the bad.

Tony Schwartz introduced the idea that voters choose candidates one of four ways, for or against either candidate. Like politicians, current employers have the incumbent advantage. They are a known quantity. Even if what they offer is less than ideal, most employees will choose to stay because it is better than the unknown future.

One of the most popular strategies we use with clients is the "stay interview." A stay interview is an intentional interview with employees to discover what keeps them around. The following are categories to cover while conducting a stay interview. The six core questions to pose while conducting the interview include:

- What is the #1 thing you love most about working here?
- When a new acquaintance asks about what you do, what do you say?
- How do you explain what our company does to your family or friends?
- What do you think we do really well here?
- Who are your favorite clients to serve?
- What kind of projects do you most enjoy working on?

These are just some of the questions you can ask to discover why your employees stay. Understanding why people stay is just as important as why they leave. Here are the six reasons why employees stay:

1. Character

Employees stay because they believe in the mission and character of the organization and trust the leadership. Mission matters, especially in a highly competitive job market. For companies, the clearer the mission, the higher the retention. Now, this does not mean you are bound to lose employees forever unless you become a non-profit. Many non-profits we work with have higher employee turnover than high-pressure sales organizations. Every organization has a mission. When the leaders forget how to involve their employees in that mission, they inevitably see a rise in turnover and disengagement.

2. Clarity

Employees stay because they understand where their career is headed and see their current job as a crucial step in their growth. Clarity of direction is essential for everyone, no matter their position on the career ladder. Most organizations take their employees for granted and assume their workforce will be there forever. Unfortunately, many learn too late that members of their organization need clarity on the direction of the organization and their career path. Organizations see a rise in voluntary turnover as soon as they begin to make significant changes. It gets worse when they don't inform their employees about what's coming. Always have an answer ready for the question, "What's next?"

3. Compensation

Employees stay because they feel their efforts are recognized and rewarded appropriately. Yes, money matters. It's not just what money can buy that keeps employees around. It's what money represents that inspires them to stay. When employees aren't compensated fairly, they feel unappreciated. That lack of appreciation turns into a leviathan of nastiness and includes bitterness, regret, and distrust. Compensation is the most basic way to show appreciation to your employees. But compensation alone will not keep them longer.

4. Commitment

Employees stay because they genuinely believe their existence in the organization is necessary for the company's success. This desire to be needed is why team dynamics matter. It's hard for an employee to walk away when they know how badly they're needed. Organizational loyalty is built fastest within teams that depend on one another. Companies that show their employees how important they are will keep them longer.

5. Complacency

Employees stay because they are comfortable where they are and want to avoid unnecessary change. Complacency isn't always a bad thing. Every organization needs to have a sturdy employee base that is reluctant to change jobs. It keeps things running when the entrepreneur-types are wanting to change things every six months. However, some employees choose to stay with you because they don't want to go through switching jobs. That can be dangerous. Not everyone who works for you should be. There are many employees on your payroll that aren't passionate, committed, or even effective. These employees would rather stay comfortable than move on to a job that makes more sense for their passions or skill sets.

6. Coaching

Leadership matters. Leadership is the reason that employees stay, but also the reason why they leave. If an employee has a good leader, they can endure tough times, challenging tasks, and workplace drama. People join people, not companies. Research shows that an employee's engagement level will be at its highest if they have a coaching relationship at their job. A coach is an individual who is committed to the employee's success and provides direction and perspective in their career.[7]

HOW TO MEASURE TURNOVER

Employee turnover is expensive.

We were talking with an executive of a medium-sized brand management company in the Northeast. They had contacted us to discuss their Millennial turnover, which had gone up significantly in the last year.

As we were discussing what had changed within the organization, this executive interrupted and said, "It's just so frustrating. We hire these kids, and then they leave a year later. We are either going to stop hiring young people or lower the salary of new employees."

Neither option sounded like a good idea if the organization was to keep growing. Not hiring young talent is not only age-discrimination, but it also hamstrings a company's growth as older employees retire. Additionally, lowering salaries deters good talent from joining your team and discourages your current employees. That crushes morale.

As we started discussing how the organization can practically cut its turnover and increase overall engagement, the executive interrupted again and stated, "What's this going to cost me?" We laughed a bit and replied, "It's not free, but what it costs is nothing close to what it already costs you to lose your employees at the rate you are now." Put another way, you can spend some money now and prevent more loss, or you can spend a lot of money later and keep having the same headaches.

The Society for Human Resource Management (SHRM) has determined that the average cost for employee turnover is around 150 percent per employee who leaves. To determine the cost of one lost employee to your organization, simply multiply their salary by 1.5. This percentage includes:

- The recruiters' time spent posting a new job and looking through applications.
- The hiring manager's time spent interviewing and following up with candidates.
- The human resources manager's time spent onboarding and enrolling the new hire in benefits.
- The manager's time spent away from their other duties training the new hire for their new role.
- The new hire's average six-month ramp-up time to become fully functional and familiar with the role.
- The new hire's time spent ramping-up into the role. The average ramp-up time is six months.

The fatigue of hiring, losing, replacing, and training employees has two costs. The hard cost is the salary and training time, which most organizations can quote from a spreadsheet (although most organizations don't even track this). The second cost is more expensive. There are soft costs associated with losing talent. Soft costs can be even more costly to the long-term success of your organization.

Here are the soft costs that the above equation does not include.

COST OF LAWSUITS

We typically think about lawsuits when an employee is dismissed, not when they choose to leave. But according to many employment attorneys, employees who voluntarily leave are a similar liability.[8]

Let's say an employee is passed up for a promotion three years in a row. After some time, the employee goes on disability for a lower back problem. While on disability, they file a discrimination lawsuit against the employer, stating that they experienced racial discrimination in the pursuit of a promotion.

The company convenes its in-house counsel to prepare for the lawsuit. The employee's manager is interviewed, briefed, and prepared. The manager's area supervisor is interviewed, briefed, and prepared. The manager and the supervisor are flown in for the deposition. The in-house counsel hires outside counsel to support the case. In all, the company has committed over 100 hours of corporate assets and nearly $1 million to this lawsuit. The company and the employee eventually settle for $500,000, and they go their separate ways.

This scenario happens every single day in America. No matter your organization's size, you cannot afford to drain your team's time or your company's profit to fight these preventable lawsuits.

COST OF DECREASED MORALE

As consultants and speakers, we travel around the world and spend countless hours in airports and at rental car counters.

A few years ago, we landed in Los Angeles to speak at a conference. If you want to see how a potential business or life partner reacts in high-stress scenarios, bring them to any Los Angeles Airport car rental facility.

After landing, we grabbed our bags and boarded the shuttle to the rental car facility. As we got off the shuttle, we were handed a ticket and told to wait until they called our number. As we looked around, we could tell this would be a while. Families were picnicking on the floor, business people were Skyping from planter boxes, and frustrated tourists were eager to start their vacations. After 15 minutes, our number was called. Finally! We thought they would help us immediately. No! We were then directed to stand in line. Yes, we had to wait outside before we could go inside and wait some more.

Another 30 minutes went by, and the line was barely moving. But then something happened. People started to leave the line after waiting for almost an hour! First one, then two, then five families got out of line and left. At first, we were thrilled (shorter line for us!). But then we started to get concerned. Did they know something we didn't?

We had to know. Brian tapped on the shoulder of the man in front of us and asked what was going on. The man said folks had started making reservations at other rental car agencies. "So the line is much shorter over there?" we asked with hope.

The man shrugged his shoulders and said he was planning on slugging it out since he had been there for almost an hour and a half. We decided to stick it out as well. After two hours, we had our rental car (not the type of car we had reserved since they were out of those, of course) and we were off to sit in Los Angeles traffic.

As we drove off into rush hour, we couldn't help but wonder, "Should we have left for a different rental car facility earlier?" We perceived that "everyone was leaving" when, in fact, only ten total families had left out of 70. But those ten families were all standing near us. Therefore, it seemed like the majority of people were making better decisions than us.

If we were standing outside and had heard that ten families left to go to another agency, we may have been curious. But at only 30 minutes in, we wouldn't have left. If you had told us as we got off the bus that ten families just left for another agency, we would have left immediately.

Why is that? The less time we invest in a situation, the more likely we are to switch to something easier or better for us. The longer we stay in a situation (a job, a relationship, or a line), the less likely we are to leave because we feel too invested.

The longer you stay, the more justifications you give for poor behavior. We could have said, "The slowly moving line is because of a heavy travel day" or, "I think it's spring break for a lot of schools, don't you?" When in reality, it could have been inadequate staffing, underdeveloped staff, or an outdated physical structure.

The hard cost of turnover doesn't count the invisible costs that can be just as lethal and lead to additional turnover. Turnover impacts the performance of the rest of the team as they see, hear, and feel every time a fellow employee quits.

When employees see others leaving, they start to question their loyalty. This doubt happens whether there is high turnover or not. Employees will begin to wonder, "Why are they leaving? Do they know something I don't? Should I be looking for another job, too?"

One unhappy employee turns into ten quickly as morale drops within the organization.

COST OF LOST PRODUCTIVITY

Here's another soft cost. It can take up to six months to properly onboard and train a new hire to proficiency. In those six months, the individual is making mistakes, learning the ropes, and getting their rhythm. But they are also causing the company to lose money. It often takes up to one year (sometimes longer) to get a new employee producing the same amount as an existing employee.

Here's how this plays out. For example, Jim just got hired to work in the sales division at Average Company Incorporated. Jim has three years of experience selling products. His first week is spent poring over product catalogs and listening to recorded sales calls of the highest and lowest performing sales representatives.

Jim then shadows a sales representative for the next four weeks, attending business luncheons and client presentations to pick up the nuances of the job. Halfway through his second month, Jim is feeling confident that he can find and close clients on his own. By month three, Jim is now leading sales calls and meetings with clients. But, he is still being shadowed by his manager to ensure quality control. It's now month four, and Jim is being recommended to begin running on his own. After a few more assessments by his supervisor, Jim becomes a full-fledged member of the sales team.

So how much did that cost? In Jim's first four months, he made two sales on his own and was a part of closing six deals. The sales Jim brought in totaled $20,000 while the sales that he observed during his training totaled $120,000. His manager typically closes ten sales per month but was only able to close six sales per month since hiring Jim. The decrease in sales was the result of observing and training Jim.

Jim's manager lost roughly 12 sales due to training Jim. Most organizations do not measure the lost time of the manager or the ramp-up time required for a new hire to be proficient in their roles. This lost manager time and ramp-up time is why retaining Jim over the long term is critical. The time and attention invested in his success are too much to go to waste.

COST OF ACQUISITION

It takes the average human resources professional 42 days to find, recruit, and interview a candidate.[9] Depending on the nature of the work and the expertise required to do the job, the time it takes to recruit can grow significantly. For example, employers looking for specialized skills can expect to lengthen their time to recruit by 6 to 12 months. Even for companies with dedicated recruiting teams, the challenge of finding employees to replace the old ones is extremely taxing.

Human resources leaders tell us they receive anywhere between 100 and 800 applications per job opening. Imagine going through that many résumés! Before you think it a waste to spend too much time recruiting, remember the cost of replacement. No one wants to find out the person they've been training for the last six months is leaving.

COST OF LEADERSHIP DISTRACTION

Have you ever hired someone only to find yourself doing both jobs a few weeks later? You're not alone. Managers report significant increases in time away from their primary duties when onboarding a new hire. A manager spends an average of one workday each week coaching new or underperforming employees.[10] That's 8 hours every week they aren't doing their job. Although it is time well spent, there are productivity ramifications.

That's 25 hours in which the manager isn't checking in, overseeing, managing, and reviewing their own work. Most organizations we work with have no idea how long it takes to onboard someone into the company. They don't factor in management time lost or the energy required. They assume it's all "part of the process." But that process costs money and opportunity.

POSITIVE TURNOVER

There is such a thing as positive turnover. Positive turnover is the kind of turnover that is good for the company and the employee. There are three types of positive turnover:

1. The Toxic Employee Leaves

This type of positive turnover happens when a disgruntled employee leaves. The voluntary or involuntary departure of a disgruntled employee is positive because their leaving is good for the overall culture of the organization. Toxic individuals infect teams, departments, and entire companies. The value of their work will never outweigh the damage of their toxicity. Leaders should never regret letting a toxic person go, even if they are a senior leader or very skilled in their work. You can train for skills. You cannot always train for ethics. When someone toxic leaves, it is important to debrief the team. Collect their perspectives on what happened and create buy-in for how the team can help rebuild the culture.

2. The Employee Leaves to Start Their Own Company

This type of positive turnover happens when an entrepreneurial employee leaves to start their own company. Celebrate this kind of turnover. Encourage them in their endeavors and help support their project where appropriate. This encouragement is wise for two reasons. If their new company doesn't make it and they return to the workforce, they may come back to you. If they continue on their own, they will remember your support and refer candidates your way.

3. The Employee Leaves for a Better Opportunity

If an employee leaves the company for a new opportunity that is better for them, put your loss aside and celebrate with them. It is essential to reflect on their opportunity and use it as a learning experience. Consider whether the opportunity was something that your organization could have provided. If not, wish the employee well. This positive attitude will come back and benefit you in the form of referrals, clients, and goodwill.

ESSENTIALS TO RETAIN THEM LONGER

No employee will quit your company without a reason. It may be lack of recognition, no opportunity to grow, or an overbearing boss. No matter the cause, it all comes down to expectations. They were expecting something that never happened, or didn't happen how they wanted. Either way, the trust bond has been broken, and they are moving on. It is essential to know why your employees

KEEP THEM LONGER

leave in order to keep them longer. It is too late to wait until the exit interview.

Ask what would be the main reason your employees would quit in anonymous engagement surveys. Invite respondents to give specific examples rather than general answers (opt for an explanation around compensation rather than asking if they just want more money). Why employees stay is different than why they leave. However, not all turnover is bad. Define what is positive turnover for your organization and celebrate individuals who move on to better opportunities.

HOW TO DO THIS

- **Categorize Your Turnover** - In addition to measuring your turnover, great organizations track why their employees quit. Is it compensation, culture, opportunity, or something else that caused them to leave? Tracking turnover is essential to keeping them longer.

- **Conduct A Stay Interview** - Great leaders know why their people stay, not just why they leave. Ask the six core questions of your team to discover their favorite part of working for you.

- **Measure Your Turnover** - Most leaders do not know how much turnover truly costs them. Utilize our "1.5x calculator" to assign a value to every employee you keep longer. Invite managers to calculate the cost of unnecessary turnover amongst their teams. The more individuals who understand the cost, the more partners you have in keeping them longer. This will equip you and your team with the knowledge necessary to invest in comprehensive retention programs.

- **Celebrate Positive Turnover** - Not all of your employees will work for you long term. Turnover is not only normal, it is healthy. When employees no longer provide value to the team or the clients, it's time to let them move on. Celebrating positive turnover empowers employees to take ownership of their careers rather than feeling obligated or trapped in a career they hate.

**TOOLS FOR
LEADERS**

"Treat every employee like they're your only employee, treat every customer like they're your only customer, treat every vendor like they're your only vendor."[1]

–Mike Lindell, Founder & CEO of My Pillow

When Mike Lindell premiered his customizable pillow in an infomercial, he was 27 months sober. The former crack-cocaine addict's story reads something like a superhero origin story. After quitting college, Mike tested out entrepreneurship with a couple of concepts. He tried carpet cleaning, card counting, and raising pigs.

He eventually got off cocaine after his dealers refused to sell him any more because Lindell was "their only hope." Though his company has experienced a meteoric rise, perhaps Mike's greatest superpower is how he leads his employees.[2] Mike admits that he still considers his company a small business, although it does more than $300 million in annual revenue.[3]

Treating your employees right comes from having the right mindset. As a former addict, Mike and his team are not afraid to cross personal and professional lines. Mike estimates anywhere between 10 and 20 percent of his employees struggle with addiction. If they have personal issues impacting their performance, he encourages them to get help and refers them to resources that personally helped him. When they get better? They have a guaranteed spot back at the company. Mike even admits that out of the 1,600 employees working at My Pillow, 500 have his personal phone number.[4]

What makes Mike's story so impactful? He showcases his story, the struggles, bad decisions, and personal pitfalls rather than presenting a carefully curated version of the past. His story and his vulnerability set the mood for the entire company.

THE MORE YOU GIVE, THE MORE THEY'LL STAY

Not every leader is prepared to give as much as Mike. There are preconceived notions about what role a manager plays in an organization. Is it to make sure everyone gets their work done? Is it to delegate tasks and manage the outcome? Is it to relay information from executives to the employees? No. It is much more than that. As we have discussed at length, leadership is influence.

This chapter is designed for executives, mid-level managers, presidents, vice presidents, and anyone seeking influence within an organization. It is designed to quickly equip you with the best practices to evaluate and implement the mindset and strategies proven to keep them longer.

DEFINING YOUR MANAGEMENT STYLE

There are three different management styles.

1. The Hands-Off Manager

A Hands-Off manager shares a goal with his or her team and walks away. The group can achieve the collective goal how and when they want. These types of managers are delegators. They trust the people around them to get the work done. The benefit of a Hands-Off manager is that he or she empowers the team to become problem solvers. Hands-Off managers allow others to be the masters of their destiny.

The challenge with Hands-Off managers is that they overlook problems that a more present leader would quickly identify. Hands-Off managers are the type to give you a directive with high expectations and little explanation.

2. The Hands-In Manager

A Hands-In manager listens to everyone's opinion and makes a final decision. They look for buy-in from the team and value mutual respect. The benefits of a Hands-In manager is increased collaboration and input. Every member of the team sees this decision-maker as caring about their perspective.

The challenge of this management style is that decisions tend to take longer. Plus, the risk of groupthink is higher. New and inexperienced leaders can fall under this type of management style. If the team doesn't know why the leader is seeking their opinion, the team might think the leader lacks the experience, judgment, and skills to make a decision.

3. Hands-On Manager

A Hands-On manager will set the course and stick around to ensure the team does it right. They are very present and, because of their experience, are available to help when problems arise. Hands-On managers are present when the team needs them the most.

On the other hand, this type of management can be dangerous when it turns into micro-managing, which erodes trust among the team. Our research shows that how you manage is influenced by how you were parented.

Were your parents hands-on, hands-off, or somewhere in between? Did they ask you to check in when you stayed out late or did they not care when you came home? Did your parents stay up and help you with your homework? Did they want to get to know your friends and learn their names? These factors influence how you lead others—whether you realize it or not.

THE TOP FIVE THINGS THAT COMPANIES CAN DO RIGHT NOW

If you've made it this far into Keep Them Longer, congratulations! You're part of the top 20 percent of all readers who make it to the end. We have intentionally designed this book to address the core needs that our clients face. Now we want to show you how to implement the principles that we have shared with you.

The steps below are how to implement "The Secret Sequence." They are how you leverage the core principles we have shared with you. Each step is designed as a series and builds upon the previous step.

One of the biggest mistakes that leaders make when reading a book like this is to extract and implement one principle or idea without context. We have done the work, developed the programs, and know what needs to be done when and in what order. Use the following five steps as a guide and a structure to build your own Keep Them Longer strategy.

STEP ONE: ASSESS THE DAMAGE

Most organizations are professional assessors but amateur problem-solvers. They're so good at measuring problems that they've forgotten how to solve them. The first step to keeping them longer is ensuring you know where the real problems are.

Start by discovering how much your turnover is costing. You must go beyond simply knowing that you're losing talent. Great companies know how much turnover costs per department and per role. You can't manage (or solve) what you don't measure.

Next, conduct strategic surveys with follow-up focus groups. Most organizations survey their employees to death. Everyone knows the problems, but very few ask those individuals who complain if they want to help make it better. Engagement surveys without follow-up focus groups are dangerous. We see a spike in turnover after traditional engagement surveys. Employees are more aware of what makes them unhappy at work, and, when nothing happens after the survey, they seek other opportunities.

Here is a quick guide to surveying your employees:

Make It as Short as Possible - No one likes spending time on a survey that they're not sure will make a difference. It takes less than five minutes to vote for the president. It doesn't take much longer than that to measure how engaged your employees are.

- **Be Careful Not to Make Everything Multiple Choice** - Asking multiple-choice questions is helpful in the short term but problematic in the long run. It limits your employees' opportunity to share their true feelings and relies on your ability to predict what they want accurately. Multiple choice questions should only be asked if you are collecting information that can be compared over years or across departments.

- **Collect the Words and Phrases Your Employees Are Using** - What employees write when they answer open-ended survey questions is incredibly valuable. "I'm frustrated at work" versus "I'm frustrated at work because my manager doesn't seem to care about my development" is very different. The words and phrases that your employees use to describe their frustrations should inform your actions, programs, and campaigns. In the aftermath of your surveys, be sure to communicate with the words and phrases that they use. How you label your solutions should mirror how they phrase the problem.

- **Empower Them to Come Up with Solutions** - Instead of just asking them to fill out a survey, empower your employees to be part of the solution. Ask your employees to share how they would make changes. Give at least two examples underneath the survey question to get their creativity going. You will be amazed at the ideas your team members are ready to share. Remember the CNX employees who saved the company millions of dollars? Consider how you can involve your employees in discovering and implementing the solution.

- **End with a Positive, Not a Negative** - Many of the engagement surveys we analyze inadvertently make the employee feel terrible about their job. The surveys pull out all of the negative things about the job, highlight every frustration, and put them in a terrible mood. Then they have to go back to work. Yuk! Restructure your surveys so your team shares how you can improve and is excited about being a part of the solution. Use the review to collect information, but also use it to remind them how great it is to work at your company.

- **Tell Them How You Plan on Using the Information** - If this is part of a scheduled engagement survey, share why you want to measure their engagement. Tell your employees if the survey is to help inform a new program, share ideas on renovating the office, or ask their feedback on benefits. If you share how the survey will be utilized, you will get more honest feedback and higher participation rates.

STEP TWO: COLLECT FEEDBACK FROM EMPLOYEES, AND LISTEN

No one wants to hear that his or her feedback isn't helpful.

We recently had a bad experience at Starbucks. We were on our way back from a conference and had another hour until we hit our town. We knew we could make the drive, but it was almost 10 p.m., and we could use some caffeine. Heck, we would have settled for a decaffeinated coffee!

We looked up the nearest coffee shop. They had all closed at least one hour before. After some heavy investigative work, we discovered there was a Starbucks near a university that we could pass through on our way home. We entered the coordinates and realized we would be arriving five minutes after their posted closing time. We would typically just bet on them staying open a few minutes later, but this was a desperate situation. We gave the store a ring, and the manager answered.

We explained the situation and asked if they would be able to stay open five minutes later for us to run in and get a quick coffee. The manager quickly responded that she locks the front door at precisely 10 p.m. No one would be allowed in. We asked if we ordered online could we have one of the employees open the door and hand it to us. We didn't even need to come inside!

Still no.

Now what we did next is only a reflection of how badly we needed coffee. In an uncaffeinated blur, we left a Google review of the poor customer service. We eventually made it home (sans coffee) and forgot about our late-night rant.

One week went by. We received an email from Google thanking us for my review and letting us know that our review has helped more than 100 customers. Wow! We just thought we were cranky about not getting coffee, but now we know that people actually read those reviews.

And you know what? We have now left more reviews of experiences at restaurants—good, bad, and indifferent—because we know that those reviews matter. No one wants to provide feedback and learn that nothing ever changed. Every one of us wants to know that our feedback matters.

The same is true with engagement surveys. You should never collect information that you do not intend to resolve. It is not only disrespectful of their time, it is disingenuous and dangerous if you want to keep them longer!

Unfortunately, corporate tradition is to bag the data and treat the results like the weather forecast. You know there is a storm coming. You don't know if the damage will be as significant as they report and yet you feel helpless to do anything.

Get your employees in on creating a solution. If you were a donut shop and all of your customer reviews said that they hated your frosting or wished there were more tables, would you ignore them? No! You would make changes right away. In the business world, lousy feedback directly translates into lost money.

Why don't employers treat their employees like customers? Next time you do an engagement survey, choose the biggest problem everyone complains about. Maybe it's the benefits package (always a touchy subject). Or perhaps it is the flexible work schedule or updating your computer system.

Put together a committee of employees who are most passionate about fixing that particular problem. Then tell them to come up with a cost-effective way of resolving the issue. After three months, let them present it to the executives and defend their approach. This level of participation allows employees at all levels to feel empowered to make a difference instead of just complaining.

STEP THREE: TRAIN LEADERS AT ALL LEVELS TO GET BUY-IN

Have you ever started a diet and your partner wasn't on board? You get the gym membership, the supplements, the $100 running shoes. You are excited about your new commitment to your health, and you come home to macaroni and cheese on the counter and your favorite ice cream in the freezer. When you go out, your partner wants to go to the grease bucket instead of the salad bar. You go to work, and it seems to be everyone's birthday with cupcakes, donuts, and soda galore.

You make it through the first few days with your enthusiasm and willpower alone. But after a while, your self-control starts to fade. You start picking at the leftover fries on your partner's plate. Then you order a small one for yourself. Before you know it, you are elbow deep into a fried food relapse.

So what happened? You were excited at the beginning, but because you didn't get everyone on board with your new direction, your willpower died out, and the familiar returned.

Studies show if you start a diet without creating a supportive environment, your results will not last.[5] The same is true when we encourage positive change within organizations. You develop a new training program, and everyone seems to be on board at first. But if you don't train the managers, supervisors, executives, and employees at all levels, the change you are adopting will not last. Your leaders will feel like hostages to change rather than partners in building the future.

STEP FOUR: DEVELOP THE PROGRAM

Your culture will not change without a program or a process. We were recently in a friend's home after they had moved in. They were newlyweds and were consolidating their furniture. The house they had just moved into was beautiful, but the former occupants had interesting wall color choices. And by interesting, I mean the walls rotated between bright pink and lavender!

Our friends ended up repainting the entire house, but they forgot one closet downstairs, which is now a very bright surprise for anyone hanging up their coat. The whole process delayed their move-in by over a month. Although it would have been faster to get their stuff in their home, they knew they wouldn't be able to make all the renovations needed if they rushed it.

Many organizations sacrifice effectiveness for efficiency. Leaders try to develop well-meaning programs and put them within the walls of an organization that isn't ready for it. Before rearranging the furniture, you need to create an appropriate structure and get it in place before starting with the accessories.

Determine what structural improvements you can make within the organization.

Here are the five things to consider:

1. **Physical** - What does the office space look like? Is it warm and inviting? Does it reflect the core culture and competencies of the organization? Does the team feel at home in the space?

2. **Compensation** - Does everyone understand the compensation structure? Do employees feel deeply disrespected or incredibly honored?

3. **Benefits** - Does everyone feel that the benefits program works for them? Do they understand how to use it? Are there alternative benefits (health incentives, etc.) that can be adopted at little or no cost?

4. **Flexibility** - Everyone wants "work-life balance." But work-life balance means something different to

every person on your team. Does your team feel empowered to get the work done in a way that respects their personal lives?

5. **Access** - Does your team feel out of the loop? Do your employees know how and why decision making affects them?

STEP FIVE: DETERMINE THE MEASUREMENT OF ACCOUNTABILITY

The average raise that an employee can expect is 3 percent. However, if an employee leaves a company, that employee can look forward to a 10 to 20 percent increase in salary.[6] Employees who stay are punished while people who leave are rewarded. It is no wonder that people are willing to move laterally to raise their standard of living!

What does success look like? Can you quantify it? If you don't measure success, you will never be able to achieve it. The companies we help have lasting impact and empower each department to quantify retention. What is a healthy level of turnover, alarming turnover, and unacceptable turnover? Does it look like a 20 percent increase in new employees staying past six months? Does it look like 30 percent of employees applying to the leadership development program?

Don't be afraid to create an accountability system that is unique to each department and developed by leaders at all levels. The more transparency you provide, the more opportunity you give employees to have buy-in into the mission.

PROGRAMS PROVEN TO CUT TURNOVER

1. Mentoring

Mentoring has been an essential aspect of career growth for centuries. Mentoring relationships exist in literature, film, and real life. Luke Skywalker had Yoda. Plato had Aristotle. Aristotle had Socrates. Some of today's most successful stars were mentored by great people. Arnold Schwarzenegger's acting coach was comedic legend Lucille Ball. Steve Jobs mentored Mark Benioff of Salesforce.com. Audrey Hepburn mentored Elizabeth Taylor.

Mentoring is essential. It helps connect new employees with established experts. It facilitates cross-generational collaboration. It preserves institutional knowledge and passes down best practices to newer individuals in the group. It celebrates the legacy and honors the time-tested expertise and experience of more senior employees.

There is a fundamental understanding of why mentoring is a powerful medium to pass knowledge through an organization. Yet only 71 percent of Fortune 500 companies report having intentional mentoring programs according to the Association of Talent Development. That may seem like a lot, but, given the stakes, simply having a program isn't enough.

Organizations of every size are experiencing the largest generational power handoff in history. Nearly 10,000 Baby Boomers turn 65 every day in America. They are retiring a decade later than previous generations. More Millennials and Gen Z are entering the workplace, expecting to train for their first job at their first job. Generation X, the often-overlooked generation in the middle, is busy honing their skills and collecting expertise for when it is their turn to lead.

We have developed mentoring programs for companies, chambers of commerce, and universities. Organizations will use our mentoring programs because they have tried it on their own and realized that excellent mentoring does not just happen. If you are like the hundreds of organizations struggling to create a culture of mentorship, there are three reasons that your mentoring program isn't working.

First, there is no training. Companies do not adequately train the mentors or mentees. You would never be expected to coach a sport that you have never played. And if you were forced to coach, you couldn't be expected to be very good. We throw mentors and mentees into relationships with one another without adequately preparing them. Mentor training doesn't have to be time-consuming; a simple 60-minute briefing will do. But it does have to be practical. You should train your mentors on how to set expectations, how to structure their mentoring sessions, and how to coach their mentees. Mentees should know how to interact with their mentors, how to honor the time investment, and how to provide value to the relationship.

The second mistake companies make is not creating a mentoring structure. When someone is asked to be a mentor, they are automatically considering the time investment. When you don't have enough time for yourself or your family, spending time with someone you don't know sounds impossible. That is why having a clear structure is essential. A mentoring structure should include how often they are to meet; it could be once a week, once a month, or as needed. The structure should include what type of mentoring is provided; it could be personal, professional, financial, or spiritual. The structure must also provide information on scheduling and communication. These may seem like simple keys to any relationship. They are. But having a clear structure that you deliver will help set up both mentor and mentee for success.

The third mistake companies make when mentoring is not involving mentoring in the culture of the company. Mentoring is powerful. It can happen in a moment or over a series of decades. It does not have to be limited to one-on-one relationships. Group mentoring can be incredibly effective, especially for busy executives.

Mentoring has to become a habit to keep them longer. Mentoring can happen vertically, where someone older and more experienced mentors someone younger and less experienced. It can happen horizontally, where peers mentor one another and help each other get ahead. It can happen in reverse, where younger or newer employees provide insight and their wisdom to those older or more experienced.

A healthy organization utilizes each kind of mentoring. Mentoring, in all of its iterations, respects the insights and brilliance of every individual and creates a culture that is continuously learning, growing, and changing.

2. Onboarding

When was the last time you updated your onboarding program? Better yet, when was the last time that you even looked at your onboarding program? Most organizations reduce onboarding down to mind-numbing orientation: health and benefits review, workplace safety training, more compliance, and giving them a computer login.

It's no wonder that one study found that 33 percent of employees decide within the first week if they want to stay at your company long term.[7] Onboarding should be the best first date your employees ever experience. It should affirm their decision to work for you and set the vision for their future at the company. A useful onboarding experience goes beyond compliance and invites the new hire to become a part of the culture.

A practical onboarding experience does the following:

- **Shares the Origin Story of the Company** - Who you are, why you do what you do, and where you came from.
- **Shares a Vision for the Future** - Where you are going and how the new employee is part of getting there.
- **Shares How the Company Works** - What the company does, how you make money, and what role each department plays in reaching a collective goal.
- **Shares How the New Hire Can Make a Difference** - What is expected of them and how they

can reach their personal and professional goals within the organization.

3. Career Pathing

Career paths are clearly defined development tracks that employees can leverage to reach their professional goals. It is a process by which your employees can take ownership of their careers, no matter their age or time with the company.

How do you develop career paths that keep them longer? Here are the top four programs that work to develop better career paths for your employees:

- **Designate a Career Concierge** - The role of career concierge is simple. They coach employees at every level of their careers. They help answer questions about the process and timelines for promotion, pay raises, and advancement. They also keep the results of every employee's *PurposeFinder Formula*™, including their passions and core skills. That way, when new opportunities pop up, they can direct them to the most qualified or most interested candidate internally.

- **Launch a Tracking Program** - Most organizations have a leadership development program for new or growing managers. That's important, but it usually ends up training people for leadership after they have become a manager. That's like getting someone up in the air and then starting flight school.

The stakes are higher at that point. Instead, have clear training tracks that employees can choose upon hiring. The track could prepare them for leadership, allow them to balance life and work better, or get them to a level of proficiency in their skill set or expertise. If there isn't a training track that exists for their professional goals, empower your employees to create their own!

- **Host an Internal Career Fair** - Most employees know very little about the rest of the company. From what they do to who they are, organizations separate their employees across departments. That can be dangerous if you want to keep them longer. An internal career fair is a great way to encourage employees to get to know one another and learn about other opportunities within the organization. And here's the thing: they don't even need to be advertising specific jobs! Use the fair as a way to encourage employees to look inside the company instead of outside for new opportunities. One company admitted they didn't want talent in one department to leave that position for a job in another department. That seemed counterintuitive. If someone is willing to leave your organization for a job inside the company, you better believe they are eager to quit for a job outside the company. Plus, it's much cheaper to make internal hires than to recruit, interview, and train someone from the outside.

- **Launch a Rotational Program** - Rotational programs are becoming very popular within organizations looking to recruit young employees. That's great. But don't stop there. Rotational programs can be great for employees at all levels. They help bring the company closer together, increase ownership amongst employees, and reduce turnover. Rotational programs are also great at mixing things up for employees who may feel stagnant or uninspired in their current positions. Whether that is rotating team members to other projects or having people move offices once a year, great things happen when you rotate talent.

YOUR VISION AND MISSION GOES BEYOND A STATEMENT

There is an ancient principle: "Without a vision, the people perish."

Walking through the halls of a typical office building, we asked one of the employees what they believed the mission of the organization was. He cocked his head a bit as he sputtered out something about serving clients with excellence and working hard. It was clear he was stringing the words together as they came out of his mouth. But when he was done, we could tell he felt somewhat pleased with himself and his creativity. We smiled, thanked him, and kept walking. Three cubicles down, we asked a young woman the same question, "What's the mission of the company here?" Her response was much more to the point: "We do public accounting."

So which is it?

Nearly every organization has a vision and mission statement. It's typically developed through hours of deliberation in poorly lit conference rooms or handed over by highly paid consultants telling you your purpose. And after all that, you take that mission statement and bury it somewhere on the "About Us" section of your website. Your employees never see it, and your customers never understand it.

A clear vision statement and compelling mission statement is the foundation of a culture that keeps them longer.

Many consultants confuse vision statements and mission statements. Here is the simplest way we have been able to differentiate the two:

Vision Statement: "What we want to achieve."

Mission Statement: "How we get there."

The five elements of an effective vision statement:

- Big Enough to Inspire
- Explains Why the Mission Is Important
- Timeless
- Has a Moral Cause
- States the Company's Role in Achieving It

The five elements of an effective mission statement:

- Extremely Clear
- Answers "What by When"
- Timeless
- Measurable
- Others-Focused

Mission and vision statements are relevant because they draw people to you. But the mission and vision statements will never keep them. That is, until each person on your team understands their individual roles in achieving the collective goal. One of the most important activities we do with clients is helping their team members write their personal mission statements. We then have them connect that statement to what the company does. Everything changes when your employees know how they personally contribute to the corporate mission.

Here are some of the mission statements of the world's top brands:

Amazon.com: "To be Earth's most customer-centric company, where customers can find and discover anything they might want to buy online, and endeavors to offer its customers the lowest possible prices."[8]

ASOS: "To become the #1 fashion destination for 20-somethings globally."[9]

Intuit: "To improve its customers' financial lives so profoundly, they couldn't imagine going back to the old way."[10]

Whole Foods: "Our purpose is to nourish people and the planet. We're a purpose-driven company that aims to set the standards of excellence for food retailers. Quality is a state of mind at Whole Foods Market."[11]

American Red Cross: "The American Red Cross prevents and alleviates human suffering in the face of emergencies by mobilizing the power of volunteers and the generosity of donors."[12]

Southwest: "The mission of Southwest Airlines is dedication to the highest quality of customer service delivered with a sense of warmth, friendliness, individual pride, and company spirit."[13]

A mission statement should be unique enough to stick and short enough to remember. Unfortunately, some of the world's biggest brands have vague and uninspiring mission statements.

Here are some profoundly disappointing mission statements from major brands:

Disney: "The mission of The Walt Disney Company is to entertain, inform and inspire people around the globe through the power of unparalleled storytelling, reflecting the iconic brands, creative minds and innovative *technologies that make ours the world's premier entertainment company.*"[14]

Sony*: "Fill the world with emotion, through the power of creativity and technology.*"[15]

Cisco*: "Shape the future of the Internet by creating unprecedented value and opportunity for our customers, employees, investors, and ecosystem partners.*"[16]

Home Depot*: "The Home Depot is in the home improvement business and our goal is to provide the highest level of service, the broadest selection of products and the most competitive prices.*"[17]

The Museum of Modern Art*: " The Museum of Modern Art is dedicated to being the foremost museum of modern art in the world.*"[18]

ESSENTIALS FOR LEADERS

Great companies happen because of great leadership. Many leaders feel frazzled and frustrated under the mound of information about what they should be doing. Transformational leadership is simple. It focuses on transforming yourself first (you cannot give what you do not have), and then transforms your employees. Great leaders give first and give often. Determine your leadership style, whether it is "hands-on," "hands-in," or "hands-off." Then determine what type of leader your employees need. Leaders who keep them longer realize that retention, culture, and engagement are all moving targets. Employees want to work where their vision and mission is aligned. A great leader works towards the success of the whole by taking ownership first, and then empowering others with ownership as well.

HOW TO DO THIS

- **Get The Right Information** - Use surveys to collect information but launch focus groups to identify early adopters and hear solutions from the team.

- **Use Your "Stay Factor"** - Discover why your employees stay with regular stay interviews and commit time and energy to do more of what makes your team proud to work for you. Stay interviews work best when done regularly (between one and two times a year) and are conducted by their direct manager or an HR representative.

- **Make Retention A Team Sport** - Get buy-in from your employees at all levels before implementing the program. This will ensure its success as well as divide labor amongst the team. The most effective strategy to get buy-in? Involve them in the design and roll out of any retention program you put together.

- **Develop Your Development** - Create clear training tracks for employees at all levels of the company and offer rotational programs that introduce employees to new opportunities within the company.

- **Make Your Vision BIG** - Big visions pull people instead of push them. Questions to ask your team: Is your vision big enough? Do people want to be a part of your story? How do you daily demonstrate your vision to your employees? How do you demonstrate your vision to job candidates? Involve your team in developing vision and mission statements that reflect your values, goals, and personality.

ABOUT THE AUTHORS

BRIAN BOSCHÉ

Brian is the CEO of The Millennial Solution and a former national journalist. He is a bestselling author and international speaker on the topics of generations and finding purpose at work. Brian and his team at The Millennial Solution help business leaders and companies (big and small) engage their talent. He has personally consulted Fortune 500 companies, A-list celebrities, and designed strategies for leaders looking to remain on top in this competitive talent market. Brian has co-hosted SiriusXM programming and been featured on NPR, The Economist, and Fox News Channel.

For Booking: MillennialSolution.com or BrianBosche.co

GABRIELLE BOSCHÉ

Gabrielle is the Founder of The Millennial Solution and is known as America's Millennial expert. She is one of the most requested speakers on generational leadership and Millennial motivation. Gabrielle is the bestselling author of three books on her generation, including: 5 *Millennial Myths: The Handbook For Managing and Motivating Millennials*. Gabrielle has co-hosted SiriusXM programming and been featured on NPR, Fox Business, Bloomberg Radio, Business Insider, Glamour, and Fast Company. Gabrielle's popular TEDx Talk discusses whether Millennials will be the next great generation. That talk has taken her to stages around the world.

For Booking: MillennialSolution.com or GabrielleBosche.com

Keep Them Longer
How To Gain, Train, And Retain Top Talent
Brian Bosché and Gabrielle Bosché

Published by Purpose Books.

RESEARCH NOTES

Chapter 1

[1] Phil is not his original name. His name was changed to protect his anonymity.

[2] Warren, R. (2013, December 31). The Purpose Driven Life: What On Earth Am I Here For? Retrieved August 27, 2019, from https://www.amazon.com/Purpose-Driven-Life-What-Earth/dp/031033750X

[3] Myths of the Modern Megachurch. (2005, May 23). Retrieved August 27, 2019, from https://www.pewforum.org/2005/05/23/myths-of-the-modern-megachurch/

Chapter 2

[1] Britannica, T. (n.d.). Bernard Palissy. Retrieved August 27, 2019, from https://www.britannica.com/biography/Bernard-Palissy

[2] Lesser, C. (2017, September 14). The Renaissance Artist Who Cast Live Snakes, Frogs, and Lizards to Make His Ceramics. Retrieved August 27, 2019, from https://www.artsy.net/article/artsy-editorial-renaissance-artist-cast-live-snakes-frogs-lizards-ceramics

[3] Oval Basin (Getty Museum). (n.d.). Retrieved August 27, 2019, from http://www.getty.edu/art/collection/objects/1196/attributed-to-bernard-palissy-oval-basin-french-about-1550/

[4] Britannica, T. (n.d.). Bernard Palissy. Retrieved August 27, 2019, from https://www.britannica.com/biography/Bernard-Palissy

[5] Dooge, J. C. (2001, May). Concepts of the Hydrological Cycle - Ancient and Modern. Retrieved August 27, 2019, from http://hydrologie.org/ACT/OH2/actes/03_dooge.pdf

[6] Samuel Slater. (n.d.). Retrieved August 27, 2019, from https://www.pbs.org/wgbh/theymadeamerica/whomade/slater_hi.html

[7] Contingent and Alternative Employment Arrangements Summary. (2018, June 07). Retrieved August 28, 2019, from https://www.bls.gov/news.release/conemp.nr0.htm

[8] Istrate, E., Ph.D., & Harris, J. (n.d.). The Future of Work: The Rise of the Gig Economy. Retrieved August 28, 2019, from https://www.naco.org/featured-resources/future-work-rise-gig-econom

[9] U.S. Bureau of Labor Statistics. (2019, August 22). Number of Jobs, Labor Market Experience, and Earnings Growth [Press release]. Retrieved August 28, 2019, from https://www.bls.gov/news.release/pdf/nlsoy.pdf

Chapter 3

[1] The Editors of Encyclopaedia Britannica (Ed.). (n.d.). Abraham Maslow. Retrieved August 28, 2019, from https://www.britannica.com/biography/Abraham-H-Maslow

[2] Maslow, A. H. (n.d.). A Theory of Human Motivation. Retrieved August 28, 2019, from https://psychclassics.yorku.ca/Maslow/motivation.htm

[3] Rutledge, P. B., Ph.D. (2011, November 8). Social Networks: What Maslow Misses. Retrieved August 28, 2019, from https://www.psychologytoday.com/us/blog/positively-media/201111/social-networks-what-maslow-misses-0

[4] Alanis Morissette: Happiness Is a Temporary State. (n.d.). Retrieved August 28, 2019, from http://www.oprah.com/own-super-soul-sunday/alanis-morissette-happiness-is-a-temporary-state-video

[5] Fitzpatrick, M. D. & Moore, T. J. (2018). The mortality effects of retirement: Evidence from Social Security eligibility at age 62. Journal of Public Economics, 157(January), 121-137.

[6] Wu C, Odden MC, Fisher GG, et al Association of retirement age with mortality: a population-based longitudinal study among older adults in the USA J Epidemiol Community Health 2016;70:917-923.

[7] McConnell, A. R., Ph.D. (2013, August 1). Belongingness: Essential Bridges that Support the Self. Retrieved August 28, 2019, from https://www.psychologytoday.com/us/blog/the-social-self/201308/belongingness-essential-bridges-support-the-self

[8] The Editors of Encyclopaedia Britannica (Ed.). (n.d.). Bo Schembechler. Retrieved August 28, 2019, from https://www.britannica.com/biography/Bo-Schembechler

[9] Schembechler, B.; Bacon, J. U. (2008). Bo's Lasting Lessons: The Legendary Coach Teaches the Timeless Fundamentals of Leadership. New York, NY: Business Plus.

[10] Diener, E., &; Chan, M. Y. (2011). Happy People Live Longer: Subjective Well-Being Contributes to Health and Longevity. Applied Psychology: Health and Well-Being, 3(1), 1-43.

[11] Konrath, S. H., & Brown, S. (2013). The effects of giving on givers.

Chapter 4

[1] Vance, R. J., Ph.D. (n.d.). Employee Engagement and Commitment: A guide to understanding, measuring and increasing engagement in your organization (Rep.). Retrieved August 28, 2019, from SHRM Foundation website: https://www.shrm.org/hr-today/trends-and-forecasting/special-reports-and-expert-views/Documents/Employee-Engagement-Commitment.pdf

[2] Employee Engagement: It's Time to Go 'All-In': Making Engagement a Daily Priority for Leaders (Issue brief). (n.d.). Dale Carnegie Research Institute.

[3] OD Network, Vogelsang, J., Ph.D., Townsend, M., Minahan, M., Jamieson, D., Vogel, J., . . . Valek, L. (n.d.). Handbook for Strategic HR - Section 5: Employee Engagement. HarperCollins Publishing. Retrieved August 28, 2019, from Amazon.com

[4] Eyal, N. (n.d.). Forming New Habits: Train to be an Amateur, Not an Expert. Retrieved August 28, 2019, from https://www.nirandfar.com/train-to-be-amateur-not-expert/

Chapter 5

[1] Pallardy, R. (n.d.). 2010 Haiti earthquake. Retrieved August 28, 2019, from https://www.britannica.com/event/2010-Haiti-earthquake

[2] Woyke, E. (2011, August 11). What The Red Cross Learned From Its Haiti Mobile Campaign. Retrieved August 28, 2019, from https://www.forbes.com/sites/elizabethwoyke/2010/08/26/what-the-red-cross-learned-from-its-haiti-mobile-campaign/#54f6dcb63462

[3] Fisher, M. (2010, August 23). 4 Reasons Why Americans Aren't Giving for Pakistan Flood Relief. Retrieved August 28, 2019, from https://www.theatlantic.com/international/archive/2010/08/4-reasons-why-americans-arent-giving-for-pakistan-flood-relief/61898/

[4] 2018 Training Industry Report (Rep.). (n.d.). Training Magazine Network.

[5] Harter, J. (n.d.). Dismal Employee Engagement Is a Sign of Global Mismanagement. Retrieved August 28, 2019, from https://www.gallup.com/workplace/231668/dismal-employee-engagement-sign-global-mismanagement.aspx

[6] Adkins, A. (2018, July 05). Millennials: The Job-Hopping Generation. Retrieved August 28, 2019, from https://www.gallup.com/workplace/231587/millennials-job-hopping-generation.aspx

[7] Toyama, K. (2015). Geek heresy: Rescuing social change from the cult of technology. New York, NY: PublicAffairs.

[8] Steindl, C., Jonas, E., Sittenthaler, S., Traut-Mattausch, E., & Greenberg, J. (2015). Understanding psychological reactance. Zeitschrift für Psychologie.

[9] Atalay, A. S., & Meloy, M. G. (2011). Retail therapy: A strategic effort to improve mood. *Psychology & Marketing, 28*(6), 638-659.

[10] Partners, E. (2017, April 27). Inside Wearables: How the science of human behavior change offers the secret to long-term engagement. Retrieved August 28, 2019, from https://medium.com/@endeavourprtnrs/inside-wearable-how-the-science-of-human-behavior-change-offers-the-secret-to-long-term-engagement-a15b3c7d4cf3

Chapter 6

[1] Guglielmo, Connie. "A Steve Jobs Moment That Mattered: Macworld, August 1997." Forbes, Forbes Magazine, 8 Oct. 2012, www.forbes.com/sites/connieguglielmo/2012/10/07/a-steve-jobs-moment-that-mattered-macworld-august-1997/#151a74f23edd.

[2] Pallardy, Richard. "Deepwater Horizon Oil Spill." Encyclopædia Britannica, Encyclopædia Britannica, Inc., www.britannica.com/event/Deepwater-Horizon-oil-spill.

[3] Baldera, A., & Guillory, R. (2019, April 15). Remembering the 9th Anniversary of the Deepwater Horizon Oil Disaster. Retrieved August 30, 2019, from https://oceanconservancy.org/blog/2019/04/15/remembering-9th-anniversary-deepwater-horizon-oil-disaster/

[4] Leaf, C., Ph.D. (2013). Switch On Your Brain: The Key To Peak Happiness, Thinking, And Health. Grand Rapids, MI: BakerBooks.

[5] Leaf, C., Ph.D. (2013). Switch On Your Brain: The Key To Peak Happiness, Thinking, And Health. Grand Rapids, MI: BakerBooks.

[6] Leaf, C., Ph.D. (2013). Switch On Your Brain: The Key To Peak Happiness, Thinking, And Health. Grand Rapids, MI: BakerBooks.

[7] Leaf, C., Ph.D. (2013). Switch On Your Brain: The Key To Peak Happiness, Thinking, And Health. Grand Rapids, MI: BakerBooks.

[8] Wagner, H. (2010, July 08). The Greatest Mathematical Discovery of All Time. Retrieved August 30, 2019, from https://www.nasdaq.com/article/the-greatest-mathematical-discovery-of-all-time-cm27783

[9] American Psychological Association. (2006, March 20). Multitasking: Switching Costs. Retrieved August 30, 2019, from https://www.apa.org/research/action/multitask

[10] Davies, R. (2018, August 02). Apple Becomes World's First Trillion-Dollar Company. Retrieved August 30, 2019, from https://www.theguardian.com/technology/2018/aug/02/apple-becomes-worlds-first-trillion-dollar-company

[11] Isaacson, W. (2013). Steve Jobs. New York, NY: Simon & Schuster.

[12] Kovach, S. (2013, February 05). Flashback: Remember When Michael Dell Said Apple Should Shut Down And Return Money To Shareholders? Retrieved August 30, 2019, from https://www.businessinsider.com/michael-dell-1997-apple-quote-2013-2

[13] Isaacson, W. (2013). Steve Jobs. New York, NY: Simon & Schuster.

[14] Guglielmo, Connie. "A Steve Jobs Moment That Mattered: Macworld, August 1997." Forbes, Forbes Magazine, 8 Oct. 2012, www.forbes.com/sites/connieguglielmo/2012/10/07/a-steve-jobs-moment-that-mattered-macworld-august-1997/#151a74f23edd.

[15] Fell, J. (2011, October 27). How Steve Jobs Saved Apple. Retrieved August 30, 2019, from https://www.entrepreneur.com/article/220604

[16] Isaacson, W. (2012, April). The Real Leadership Lessons of Steve Jobs. Retrieved August 30, 2019, from https://hbr.org/2012/04/the-real-leadership-lessons-of-steve-jobs

[17] Fell, J. (2011, October 27). How Steve Jobs Saved Apple. Retrieved August 30, 2019, from https://www.entrepreneur.com/article/220604

Chapter 7

[1] Wang, A. B. (2018, November 14). When 'hell moved in,' a California nurse drove through fire to save lives. Retrieved August 30, 2019, from https://beta.washingtonpost.com/lifestyle/2018/11/14/when-hell-moved-california-nurse-drove-through-fire-save-lives/?noredirect=on

[2] Associated Press. (2019, January 08). California wildfire was world's costliest natural disaster in 2018, insurer says. Retrieved August 30, 2019, from https://www.nbcnews.com/news/us-news/california-wildfire-was-world-s-costliest-natural-disaster-2018-insurer-n956376

[3] Wang, A. B. (2018, November 14). When 'hell moved in,' a California nurse drove through fire to save lives. Retrieved August 30, 2019, from https://beta.washingtonpost.com/lifestyle/2018/11/14/when-hell-moved-california-nurse-drove-through-fire-save-lives/?noredirect=on

[4] Wang, A. B. (2018, November 14). When 'hell moved in,' a California nurse drove through fire to save lives. Retrieved August 30, 2019, from https://beta.washingtonpost.com/lifestyle/2018/11/14/when-hell-moved-california-nurse-drove-through-fire-save-lives/?noredirect=on

[5] Rogers, E., Ph.D. (2003). Diffusion of Innovations (5th ed.). New York, NY: Free Press.

[6] Rogers, E., Ph.D. (2003). Diffusion of Innovations (5th ed.). New York, NY: Free Press.

[7] Rogers, E., Ph.D. (2003). Diffusion of Innovations (5th ed.). New York, NY: Free Press.

[8] Rogers, E., Ph.D. (2003). Diffusion of Innovations (5th ed.). New York, NY: Free Press.

[9] Rogers, E., Ph.D. (2003). Diffusion of Innovations (5th ed.). New York, NY: Free Press.

[10] Rogers, E., Ph.D. (2003). Diffusion of Innovations (5th ed.). New York, NY: Free Press.

[11] Maxwell, J. C. (2007). The 21 Irrefutable Laws of Leadership: Follow Them and People Will Follow You (2nd ed.). Nashville, TN: Thomas Nelson.

[12] Banfield, E. C. (2003). Political Influence (1st ed.). New Brunswick, NJ: Transaction.

[13] Brandon, J. (2015, April 10). 20 Marissa Mayer Quotes on Making Smart Business Choices. Retrieved August 30, 2019, from https://www.inc.com/john-brandon/20-marissa-mayer-quotes-on-making-smart-business-choices.html

[14] Saad, L. (2017, December 20). Eight in 10 Americans Afflicted by Stress. Retrieved August 30, 2019, from https://news.gallup.com/poll/224336/eight-americans-afflicted-stress.aspx

[15] Carroll, Lewis. Alice's Adventures in Wonderland & Through the Looking-Glass. 1st ed., Bantam Classics, 1984.

Chapter 8

[1] Gupta, S., & Mittal, S. (2013). Yawning and its physiological significance. International Journal of Applied and Basic Medical Research, 3(1), 11.

[2] Gupta, S., & Mittal, S. (2013). Yawning and its physiological significance. International Journal of Applied and Basic Medical Research, 3(1), 11.

[3] Romero, T., Konno, A., & Hasegawa, T. (2013). Familiarity bias and physiological responses in contagious yawning by dogs support link to empathy. PloS one, 8(8), e71365.

[4] Fast, N. J., & Tiedens, L. Z. (2010). Blame contagion: The automatic transmission of self-serving attributions. Journal of Experimental Social Psychology, 46(1), 97-106.

[5] Steinberg, A. (2005, November 21). Losing Propositions. Retrieved August 30, 2019, from https://www.washingtonexaminer.com/weekly-standard/losing-propositions

[6] Blowing up the boxes. (2005, November 03). Retrieved August 30, 2019, from https://www.economist.com/special-report/2005/11/03/blowing-up-the-boxes

[7] Fast, N. J., & Tiedens, L. Z. (2010). Blame contagion: The automatic transmission of self-serving attributions. Journal of Experimental Social Psychology, 46(1), 97-106.

[8] Bright Sun Films (Director). (2018, January 26). The Story Of The Costa Concordia [Video file]. Retrieved August 30, 2019, from https://www.youtube.com/watch?v=EgTOq-2acT0

[9] Tikkanen, A. (n.d.). Costa Concordia Disaster. Retrieved August 30, 2019, from https://www.britannica.com/event/Costa-Concordia-disaster

[10] Tikkanen, A. (n.d.). Costa Concordia Disaster. Retrieved August 30, 2019, from https://www.britannica.com/event/Costa-Concordia-disaster

[11] Tikkanen, A. (n.d.). Costa Concordia Disaster. Retrieved August 30, 2019, from https://www.britannica.com/event/Costa-Concordia-disaster

[12] Squires, N. (2014, December 02). Costa Concordia captain denies performing risky 'salute' to impress his lover. Retrieved August 30, 2019, from https://www.telegraph.co.uk/news/worldnews/europe/italy/11269028/Costa-Concordia-captain-denies-performing-risky-salute-to-impress-his-lover.html

[13] Tikkanen, A. (n.d.). Costa Concordia Disaster. Retrieved August 30, 2019, from https://www.britannica.com/event/Costa-Concordia-disaster

[14] Tikkanen, A. (n.d.). Costa Concordia Disaster. Retrieved August 30, 2019, from https://www.britannica.com/event/Costa-Concordia-disaster

[15] BBC. (2015, February 10). Costa Concordia: What Happened. Retrieved August 30, 2019, from https://www.bbc.com/news/world-europe-16563562

[16] Tikkanen, A. (n.d.). Costa Concordia Disaster. Retrieved August 30, 2019, from https://www.britannica.com/event/Costa-Concordia-disaster

[17] Tikkanen, A. (n.d.). Costa Concordia Disaster. Retrieved August 30, 2019, from https://www.britannica.com/event/Costa-Concordia-disaster

[18] Tikkanen, A. (n.d.). Costa Concordia Disaster. Retrieved August 30, 2019, from https://www.britannica.com/event/Costa-Concordia-disaster

[19] Tikkanen, A. (n.d.). Costa Concordia Disaster. Retrieved August 30, 2019, from https://www.britannica.com/event/Costa-Concordia-disaster

[20] Associated Press. (2012, January 17). Costa Concordia transcript: Coastguard orders captain to return to stricken ship. Retrieved August 30, 2019, from https://www.theguardian.com/world/2012/jan/17/costa-concordia-transcript-coastguard-captain

[21] Tikkanen, A. (n.d.). Costa Concordia Disaster. Retrieved August 30, 2019, from https://www.britannica.com/event/Costa-Concordia-disaster

[22] Associated Press. (2015, January 24). Prosecutor: Captain's negligence behind 32 deaths aboard Concordia. Retrieved August 30, 2019, from https://www.japantimes.co.jp/news/2015/01/24/world/crime-legal-world/prosecutor-captains-negligence-behind-32-deaths-aboard-concordia/#.XWlasZNKhR0

[23] Reuters. (2014, July 06). Costa Concordia capsizing costs over $2 billion for owners. Retrieved August 30, 2019, from https://www.reuters.com/article/italy-concordia-costs/costa-concordia-capsizing-costs-over-2-billion-for-owners-idUSL6N0PH0EO20140706

[24] Tikkanen, A. (n.d.). Costa Concordia Disaster. Retrieved August 30, 2019, from https://www.britannica.com/event/Costa-Concordia-disaster

[25] George Washington Carver Quotes. (n.d.). Retrieved August 30, 2019, from https://www.brainyquote.com/quotes/george_washington_carver_158549

[26] Evans, N. (2013, November 13). Costa Concordia captain's mistress reveals late night sex sessions in cabin before doomed cruise liner sank. Retrieved August 30, 2019, from https://www.mirror.co.uk/news/world-news/costa-concordia-captains-mistress-reveals-2786644

[27] Lowe, K. (2009, November 24). People Like to Play the Blame Game. Retrieved August 30, 2019, from https://news.usc.edu/32055/people-like-to-play-the-blame-game/

[28] Myers, D. G., Bach, P. J., & Schreiber, F. B. (1974). Normative and informational effects of group interaction. Sociometry, 275-286.

[29] Baumeister, R. F., Zhang, L., & Vohs, K. D. (2004). Gossip as cultural learning. *Review of general psychology*, 8(2), 111-121.

[30] Baumeister, R. F., Zhang, L., & Vohs, K. D. (2004). Gossip as cultural learning. *Review of general psychology*, 8(2), 111-121.

[31] Brown, L. H., Silvia, P. J., Myin-Germeys, I., & Kwapil, T. R. (2007). When the need to belong goes wrong: The expression of social anhedonia and social anxiety in daily life. *Psychological Science*, 18(9), 778-782.

[32] Fast, N. J., & Tiedens, L. Z. (2010). Blame contagion: The automatic transmission of self-serving attributions. Journal of Experimental Social Psychology, 46(1), 97-106.

Chapter 9

[1] "Remembering Names." Dale Carnegie Training, www.dalecarnegie.com/en/courses/remember-names-new-jersey-northern-classroom.

[2] Dictionary.com. (n.d.). Purpose. Retrieved August 30, 2019, from https://www.dictionary.com/browse/purpose

[3] Dictionary.com. (n.d.). Passion. Retrieved August 30, 2019, from https://www.dictionary.com/browse/passion

[4] Casserly, M. (2013, June 19). Women, Work & Weddings. Retrieved August 30, 2019, from https://www.forbes.com/2010/07/22/wedding-planning-the-knot-wedding-channel-websites-forbes-woman-time-working-brides-survey.html#1c161f5a3af8

Chapter 10

[1] QSR. (2014, September 11). Remembering Truett Cathy. Retrieved August 30, 2019, from https://www.qsrmagazine.com/exclusives/remembering-truett-cathy

[2] DeFrank, R. S., & Cooper, C. L. (2013). Worksite stress management interventions: Their effectiveness and conceptualisation. In From Stress to Wellbeing Volume 2 (pp. 3-13). Palgrave Macmillan, London.

[3] Batman, D., Ph.D., Sackett, O., Ph.D. (n.d.). Clocking On And Checking Out (Issue brief). Virgin Pulse Global Challenge.

[4] Turvey, M. D., & Olsen, D. H. (2006). Marriage and family wellness: Corporate America's business? Minneapolis, MN: Life Innovations

[5] Kessler, R. C., Ames, M., Hymel, P. A., Loeppke, R., McKenas, D. K., Richling, D. E., ... & Ustun, T. B. (2004). Using the World Health Organization Health and Work Performance Questionnaire (HPQ) to evaluate the indirect workplace costs of illness. Journal of Occupational and Environmental Medicine, 46(6), S23-S37.

[6] Gallup (Ed.). (2017). State of the Global Workplace (Rep.). Washington, D.C..

[7] Gallup (Ed.). (2017). State of the Global Workplace (Rep.). Washington, D.C..

[8] Gallup (Ed.). (2017). State of the Global Workplace (Rep.). Washington, D.C..

[9] Muller-Heyndyk, R. (2018, September 05). Generation X men most unhappy at work. Retrieved August 30, 2019, from https://www.hrmagazine.co.uk/article-details/generation-x-men-most-unhappy-at-work

Chapter 11

[1] Tredgold, G. (2016, June 01). 49 Quotes That Will Help Boost Your Accountability. Retrieved August 30, 2019, from https://www.inc.com/gordon-tredgold/49-quotes-that-will-help-you-avoid-the-blame-game.html

[2] Estrin, J. (2015, August 12). Kodak's First Digital Moment. Retrieved August 30, 2019, from https://lens.blogs.nytimes.com/2015/08/12/kodaks-first-digital-moment/

[3] Trenholm, R. (2007, November 05). Photos: The history of the digital camera. Retrieved August 30, 2019, from https://www.cnet.com/news/photos-the-history-of-the-digital-camera/

[4] Estrin, J. (2015, August 12). Kodak's First Digital Moment. Retrieved August 30, 2019, from https://lens.blogs.nytimes.com/2015/08/12/kodaks-first-digital-moment/

[5] Estrin, J. (2015, August 12). Kodak's First Digital Moment. Retrieved August 30, 2019, from https://lens.blogs.nytimes.com/2015/08/12/kodaks-first-digital-moment/

[6] Gallup (Ed.). (2017). State of the Global Workplace (Rep.). Washington, D.C..

[7] Gallup (Ed.). (2017). State of the Global Workplace (Rep.). Washington, D.C..

[8] Jachimowicz, J. M., Chafik, S., Munrat, S., Prabhu, J. C., & Weber, E. U. (2017). Community trust reduces myopic decisions of low-income individuals. *Proceedings of the National Academy of Sciences, 114*(21), 5401-5406.

[9] Jachimowicz, J. M., Chafik, S., Munrat, S., Prabhu, J. C., & Weber, E. U. (2017). Community trust reduces myopic decisions of low-income individuals. *Proceedings of the National Academy of Sciences, 114*(21), 5401-5406.

[10] Jachimowicz, J. M., Chafik, S., Munrat, S., Prabhu, J. C., & Weber, E. U. (2017). Community trust reduces myopic decisions of low-income individuals. *Proceedings of the National Academy of Sciences, 114*(21), 5401-5406.

Chapter 12

[1] Sanahori, S. (2016, August 11). Woman gives away organ meant for her to save stranger. Retrieved August 30, 2019, from https://www.usatoday.com/story/news/humankind/2016/08/11/woman-gives-away-organ-meant-her-save-stranger/88066000/

[2] Sanahori, S. (2016, August 11). Woman gives away organ meant for her to save stranger. Retrieved August 30, 2019, from https://www.usatoday.com/story/news/humankind/2016/08/11/woman-gives-away-organ-meant-her-save-stranger/88066000/

[3] Sanahori, S. (2016, August 11). Woman gives away organ meant for her to save stranger. Retrieved August 30, 2019, from https://www.usatoday.com/story/news/humankind/2016/08/11/woman-gives-away-organ-meant-her-save-stranger/88066000/

[4] Kruse, K. (2012, November 28). Zig Ziglar: 10 Quotes That Can Change Your Life. Retrieved August 30, 2019, from https://www.forbes.com/sites/kevinkruse/2012/11/28/zig-ziglar-10-quotes-that-can-change-your-life/#7f37568226a0

[5] Tusche, A., Böckler, A., Kanske, P., Trautwein, F. M., & Singer, T. (2016). Decoding the charitable brain: empathy, perspective taking, and attention shifts differentially predict altruistic giving. Journal of Neuroscience, 36(17), 4719-4732.

[6] Janus, K. K. (2017, November 1). Innovating Philanthropy. Retrieved August 30, 2019, from https://ssir.org/articles/entry/innovating_philanthropy#

[7] Babson College. (2015, July 9). New Study, Commissioned by Verizon, Addresses a Persistent Knowledge Gap by Analyzing the Financial Impacts of Corporate Responsibility Programs. Retrieved August 30, 2019, from https://www.babson.edu/about/news-events/babson-announcements/babson-io-sustainability-release-project-roi/

[8] A History of Modern Philanthropy. (n.d.). Retrieved August 30, 2019, from https://www.historyofgiving.org/1500-1750/1580-private-benefactors-surface-in-china/

[9] Lilly Family School of Philanthropy. (2017). Giving USA 2017: The Annual Report on Philanthropy for the Year 2016 (Rep.). Chicago, IL: Giving USA.

[10] How It Works for Companies. (n.d.). Retrieved August 30, 2019, from https://www.catchafire.org/howitworks/companies/casestudies

[11] IU Lilly Family School of Philanthropy News. (2016, May 19). Retrieved August 30, 2019, from https://philanthropy.iupui.edu/news-events/news-item/parents,-grandparents-influence-charitable-giving-and-volunteering-of-children?id=199

Chapter 13

[1] Amazon.com. (2018, November 13). Amazon selects New York City and Northern Virginia for new headquarters [Press release]. Retrieved September 1, 2019, from https://blog.aboutamazon.com/company-news/amazon-selects-new-york-city-and-northern-virginia-for-new-headquarters

[2] Goodman, J. (2019, February 14). Amazon pulls out of planned New York City headquarters. Retrieved September 01, 2019, from https://www.nytimes.com/2019/02/14/nyregion/amazon-hq2-queens.html

[3] Capriel, J. (2019, March 28). Lots of job openings, not enough workers and HQ2 on the way has Fairfax County on edge. Retrieved September 01, 2019, from https://www.bizjournals.com/washington/news/2019/03/28/lots-of-job-openings-not-enough-workers-and-hq2-on.html

[4] Mind The Workplace (p. 9, Rep.). (2017). Alexandria, VA: Mental Health America.

[5] Overly, S. (2017, February 25). RIP LivingSocial: The fast rise and slow demise of a daily deals company. Retrieved September 01, 2019, from https://www.washingtonpost.com/news/innovations/wp/2017/02/25/rip-livingsocial-the-fast-rise-and-slow-demise-of-a-daily-deals-company/

[6] Scott, S. B., Rhoades, G. K., Stanley, S. M., Allen, E. S., & Markman, H. J. (2013). Reasons for divorce and recollections of premarital intervention: Implications for improving relationship education. Couple and Family Psychology: Research and Practice, 2(2), 131.

[7] Ramsey, D. (2011). EntreLeadership: 20 Years of Practical Business Wisdom from the Trenches. Brentwood, TN: Howard Books.

[8] Thurman, S., Ph.D. (2015). NSHSS Scholar 2015 Millennial Career Survey Results (Rep.). Atlanta, GA: The National Society of High School Scholars.

[9] 2018 US Survey on Absence and Disability Management (Rep.). (2018). New York City, NY: Mercer.

Chapter 14

[1] Rife, L. (2018, May 6). Carilion President and CEO Nancy agee will lead American Hospital Association board. Retrieved September 01, 2019, from https://www.roanoke.com/business/carilion-president-and-ceo-nancy-agee-will-lead-american-hospital/article_ae91430d-4486-5431-99a4-17e48c6020de.html

[2] How Millennials Want to Work and Live (Rep.). (2016). Washington, D.C.: Gallup.

[3] Ringo, J. L. (1991). Neuronal interconnection as a function of brain size. Brain, Behavior and Evolution, 38(1), 1-6.

[4] Johnson, M. H. (2002). Brain Development and Cognition: A Reader (2nd ed.) (Y. Munakata &; R. O. Gilmore, Eds.). Hoboken, NJ: Wiley-Blackwell.

[5] Knowles, M. S. (1975). Self-directed learning: A guide for learners and teachers (Vol. 2, No. 2, p. 135). New York: Association Press.

[6] Employee stress can cost companies billions. (2019, March 8). Retrieved September 01, 2019, from https://www.coloniallife.com/employer-resource-center/2019/march/employee-stress-can-cost-companies-billions

Chapter 15

[1] PBS (Producer). (1984, September 19). The 30-second President [Video file]. Retrieved September 1, 2019, from https://billmoyers.com/content/30-second-president/

[2] PBS (Producer). (1984, September 19). The 30-second President [Video file]. Retrieved September 1, 2019, from https://billmoyers.com/content/30-second-president/

[3] Goler, L., Gale, J., Harrington, B., & Grant, A. (2018, January 11). Why People Really Quit Their Jobs. Retrieved September 01, 2019, from https://hbr.org/2018/01/why-people-really-quit-their-jobs

[4] Your best employees are leaving. But is it personal or practical? (n.d.). Retrieved September 01, 2019, from https://www.randstadusa.com/about/news/your-best-employees-are-leaving-but-is-it-personal-or-practical/

[5] Beck, R., & Harter, J. (2015, April 21). Managers account for 70% of variance in employee engagement. Retrieved September 01, 2019, from https://news.gallup.com/businessjournal/182792/managers-account-variance-employee-engagement.aspx

[6] Robison, J. (2008, May 8). Turning Around Employee Turnover. Retrieved September 01, 2019, from https://news.gallup.com/businessjournal/106912/turning-around-your-turnover-problem.aspx

[7] Hicks, B., Carter, A., & Sinclair, A. (2013). Impact of coaching on employee well-being, engagement and job satisfaction. Brighton (England).

[8] LaFlamme, R. (2017, May 16). Employer sued for workers' comp a year after employee quit job. Retrieved September 01, 2019, from http://www.ennisbritton.com/blog/2017/employer-sued-workers-comp-year-employee-quit-job

[9] 2016 Human Capital Benchmarking Report (Rep.). (2016). Alexandria, VA: Society For Human Resource Management.

[10] Robert Half. (2018, May 15). The High Price Of A Low Performer [Press release]. Retrieved September 1, 2019, from http://rh-us.mediaroom.com/2018-05-15-The-High-Price-Of-A-Low-Performer

Chapter 16

[1] Pilon, A. (2019, January 11). 10 Amazing Tips to Success from Mike Lindell, the My Pillow Guy. Retrieved September 01, 2019, from https://smallbiztrends.com/2018/12/tips-to-success-mike-lindell.html

[2] Fordham, E. (2018, October 13). MyPillow CEO Mike Lindell Talks US Addiction Problem, Giving 'Second Chances'. Retrieved September 01, 2019, from https://dailycaller.com/2018/10/13/mypillow-mike-lindell-opioid-addiction-second-chance/

[3] Wells, J. (2018, January 24). How this entrepreneur went from a crack addict to a self-made multimillionaire. Retrieved September 01, 2019, from https://www.cnbc.com/2017/09/20/how-mypillow-founder-went-from-crack-addict-to-self-made-millionaire.html

[4] Fordham, E. (2018, October 13). MyPillow CEO Mike Lindell Talks US Addiction Problem, Giving 'Second Chances'. Retrieved September 01, 2019, from https://dailycaller.com/2018/10/13/mypillow-mike-lindell-opioid-addiction-second-chance/

[5] Haas, S., M.D. (2018, August 13). How to Set Up Your Environment to Help You Lose Weight. Retrieved September 01, 2019, from https://www.psychologytoday.com/us/blog/prescriptions-life/201808/how-set-your-environment-help-you-lose-weight

[6] Strauss, G. (2013, September 18). Pay raises in 2014 expected to average 3%. Retrieved September 01, 2019, from https://www.usatoday.com/story/money/personalfinance/2013/09/18/how-much-of-a-pay-raise-can-you-expect-in-2014/2832791/

[7] Center for Generational Kinetics. (2015). Is There Really A Generational Divide at Work? (Issue brief). Weston, FL: Ultimate Software.

[8] Amazon Jobs. (n.d.). Retrieved September 01, 2019, from https://www.amazon.jobs/en/working/working-amazon

[9] ASOS. (n.d.). Retrieved September 01, 2019, from https://www.asosplc.com/

[10] Intuit. (n.d.). Retrieved September 01, 2019, from https://www.intuit.com/company/

[11] Whole Foods Market. (n.d.). Retrieved September 01, 2019, from https://www.wholefoodsmarket.com/our-mission-values

[12] American Red Cross. (n.d.). Retrieved September 01, 2019, from https://www.redcross.org/about-us/who-we-are/mission-and-values.html

[13] Southwest Airlines. (n.d.). Retrieved September 01, 2019, from https://www.southwest.com/html/about-southwest/index.html

[14] The Walt Disney Company. (n.d.). Retrieved September 01, 2019, from https://www.thewaltdisneycompany.com/about/

[15] Sony. (n.d.). Retrieved September 01, 2019, from https://www.sony.net/SonyInfo/

[16] Pratap, A. (2017, July 08). Mission and Vision of Cisco: An Analysis. Retrieved September 01, 2019, from https://notesmatic.com/2017/01/cisco-mission-and-vision-analysis/

[17] The Home Depot. (n.d.). Retrieved September 01, 2019, from https://ir.homedepot.com/investor-resources/faqs

[18] The Museum of Modern Art. (n.d.). Retrieved September 01, 2019, from https://www.moma.org/about/who-we-are/moma

Made in the
USA
Lexington, KY